CHA...
THE ENERGY OF LIFE

This book teaches you how to shift your focus away from the problem mindset and, instead, focus on realigning with the inner energy—or chakra—that is causing the imbalance.

The chakras, vortexes of energy, serve as a map of your inner world. The more freely energy flows within you, the stronger your state of health and well-being.

CHAKRAS
THE ENERGY OF LIFE

Balancing Your Chakra Energies

DAVID POND

New Age Books

ISBN: 81-7822-085-7

First Indian Edition: 2002

Third Printing: USA, 2001
(Published under the title "Chakras for Beginners"
by Llewellyn Publications, USA)

© 2000 by David Pond

All rights reserved. No part of this publication may be reproduced
or transmitted in any form or by any means, electronic or mechanical, including
photocopying, recording, or by any information storage and retrieval system,
without permission in writing from the publishers.

Published by
NEW AGE BOOKS
A-44 Naraina Phase-I
New Delhi-110 028 (INDIA)
Email: nab@vsnl.in
Website: www.newagebooksindia.com

For Sale in Southeast Asia Only

Printed in India
at Shri Jainendra Press
A-45 Naraina Phase-I, New Delhi-110 028

Dedication

*To my children and their children:
David Jr., Eden, Skylar, Forest, Tawny, Coral, and Hunter.
The love we all share has been a constant source
of inspiration and meaning in my life.*

Contents

Acknowledgments / ix
Preface / xi

Section I: Introduction

The Chakras: the Energy of Life / 3
Balance / 9
Surrender / 15
Cleaning the Windows / 17

Section II: The Chakras

The Urge for Survival:
Your First Chakra / 23

The Pursuit of Pleasure:
Your Second Chakra / 33

The Drive for Power:
Your Third Chakra / 45

The Quest for Love:
Your Fourth Chakra / 55

The Voice of Creative Expression:
Your Fifth Chakra / 71

The Desire for Transcendence:
Your Sixth Chakra / 83

The Surrender to Spirituality:
Your Seventh Chakra / 101

Section III: Essays

The Dance of Ego, Soul, and Spirit / 115
Vows and the Chakras / 119
Transmuting Energy / 123
Adversary vs. Visionary Views / 127
Playing the Synthesizer of Your Being / 131
Stages of Prayer / 135
Worry as Energy / 137
Honoring Your Energy / 141
Kundalini / 143
A Myth / 145

Section IV: Exercises and Meditations

Visualization Exercise / 151
Chakra Meditation / 153
Heaven and Earth Meditation / 157

Appendix: Chakra Chart / 159
References and Suggested Reading / 163
Index / 167

Acknowledgments

THE MATERIAL IN this book is a distillation of being a seeker on the path of consciousness growth for nearly thirty years. To name all those who contributed to my understanding of the material presented in this book would be quite impossible. So I would like to express my deep gratitude collectively for the teachers, mystics, gurus, and philosophers of all ages who have left a legacy of their wisdom in books and on tapes so that we may benefit from their experiences. I would also like to express my gratitude for the community of seekers who have always been there as a tremendous resource—so many of the nuggets of wisdom I've gained in this life have come through fellow searchers of the truth.

To my first teacher on the path, my sister, Lucy Pond—thank you for opening my eyes. My yoga teacher and good friend, Bob Smith, deserves special recognition. His knowledge of the pathways that connect the chakras is unsurpassed. Through his workshops, I learned many of the techniques, postures, breath exercises, and meditations that contribute to my understanding of the chakras.

I would especially like to acknowledge my close friends, Julie and Robert Grattan. They gave helpful advice on the manuscript itself, but more than that, their belief in me and the material gave confidence and strength. Linda Joy Stone, Alex Holland, and Geri Froomer read the manuscript and offered insights into the material and editorial ideas. My wonderful mother, Mama Jane, blessed the book with her acceptance statement: "I think you have something here." I would especially like to acknowledge my close friend Lynn Mitchell. Her careful attention to the manuscript helped bring the work into its ultimate form. I would also like to thank Robert Marritz for his editorial ideas and encouragement.

I would like to thank Nancy Mostad, acquisitions manager at Llewellyn, for her support, encouragement, and personal touch in her dealings with me. I greatly appreciated meeting Carl and Sandra Weschcke, the guiding forces at Llewellyn, and discussing the book with them. They both extended a warm interest in who I am and what I have to say. I was fortunate to be able to work with editor Michael Maupin. His genuine interest in the material allowed him to make very useful suggestions and made working with him very enjoyable. I would also like to thank William Merlin Cannon for creating a cover design that accurately reflects the spirit of the book.

I would like to extent my gratitude for my artist friend Jim Sorenson, who created a beautiful working cover for the book early in the project.

Finally, my loving wife Laura's role in the book could not be overstated. Her support and encouragement throughout the project was immense. She also was willing to experiment with the exercises and activities suggested for each of the chakras and gave invaluable feedback as to what was most effective. Thank you Laura for being by my side—throughout the project and as my life partner.

Preface

WE ALL WANT the same things out of life—happiness, fulfillment, health and well-being, and satisfying relationships. It shouldn't be so hard—it all looks so simple. But things get in the way. Life happens. We know when we are unbalanced—we can feel that! But what to *do* about it?

We've been taught so much about how to develop the skills necessary for fitting into the world. It is assumed that if everything is going well for you in the outer world, you'll be happy. This is "putting the cart before the horse." We need to learn how to be happy and fulfilled at the inner level, then our outer world will fall into place as a reflection of our inner world. We need maps for sorting out these issues and achieving our birthright. The chakras can provide such a map for activating and balancing the various levels of life experiences.

The chakras are spinning vortexes of energy located just in front of the spine and positioned from the tailbone to the crown of the head. The chakras are a map of your inner world—your relationship to yourself and how you experience energy. Life is energy. The same force that flows through all of life flows through you. This is the manna—

the breath—the prana, the chi (Qi) of life. The chakras interact with this universal life force and animate the various aspects of your life, from the universal—through the individual and into earth—and then back again.

We have understood the chakras for a long time, dating back to ancient India and the Hindu yogis. But one needn't be a yogi to benefit from their insights. The ancient model has withstood the test of time because of its authenticity and its applicability. All seekers on the path eventually become aware of the chakras because of their universality.

This is not an intellectual model; it is experiential. This is not merely something to study—it's your energy! It is something with which to identify—they are your chakras. They are already operating at one level or another. Come to know the chakras within yourself, not on these pages. This is not material to memorize . . . challenge yourself to identify each of these centers within you.

My path of discovering the chakras and their value in my life was rather circuitous. I grew up fairly skilled in sports and much of my early identity was a spin-off of that focus, or at least my outer identity was. This led to a fair amount of popularity and acceptance. But on the inside I was a mess. I had a huge inner world, but didn't understand it. I had no frame of reference.

I grew up believing that since my inner world was so inconsistent with my outer world, and I was thinking about things that the outer world never addressed, something must be wrong. I was concerned for my mental well-being, but managed to keep it a secret.

I went on to college to become a schoolteacher and was again accepted by the world for my aspirations. Everything looked perfect in the outer world. However, my inner world was even more in turmoil. I followed all the steps that were supposed to lead to happiness, but I was still confused.

I was fortunate to have an astrologer for my sister and she gave me my first horoscope reading when I was twenty. Lights came on: I found a reference to my inner world that was not based on a pathological model. Astrology gave me a map to my inner world and, for the first time, I had a healthy reference for this part of my character. This opened up a spiritual quest in me and I was led to Ram Dass's book *Be Here Now*, revealing more healthy models of my inner world. I began to see this inner world as a wonderful resource rather than a source of turmoil. I was led to study the chakras, as most people on a path of self-discovery do. You hear about them on your journey of awakening.

That was nearly thirty years ago and my involvement with the chakras has been continuous ever since. They always have application. There is never a time when it is not beneficial to have a map of the two levels of being: first, what you are outwardly doing; and second, where you are at within yourself *while* you do what you are doing.

At level one, you wash the dishes. At level two, where are you within yourself *as* you wash the dishes? Are you angry, irritated, dutiful, absent-minded, peaceful, reverent? The range is practically unlimited. Just the one activity, but what a range of potential places to be within yourself as you're doing the activity! This what the chakras address, where you are within yourself as you do what you do.

I eventually completed my training as a teacher, but felt too constrained within the educational system. I needed to explore beyond the traditional walls of education. I moved my young family to Hawaii, and we lived in a commune where the University of the Universe provided an abundance of information for looking at life outside of traditional beliefs. I became an astrologer and an avid student of the mystical path.

We moved to central Washington state, started another commune and a restaurant, and continued exploring alternative lifestyles: yoga, meditation, astrology, natural foods, cooperative living. By my mid-thirties, I wanted a stiffer grid to test the metaphysical beliefs that were guiding my life and was ready to head back into academia and pursue a Master's degree. I pursued an Individualized Studies program and eventually received a Master of Science degree in Experimental Metaphysics from Central Washington University.

I was required to get approval from my committee on the course of study I created. They helped me to design my studies to meet the academic standards of the university. The courses I designed were "Jungian Psychology and Metaphysics," "Non-Traditional Healing," "The I–Ching," and "Models of Consciousness." My thesis used astrological birthcharts in comparison to traditional personality tests (The Stanford, MMPI, Meyers–Briggs, etc.). I set up an experiment and showed that astrologers were able to use birthcharts to accurately match, beyond the chance level, personality questionnaires filled out by individuals and their correct horoscope. I hoped somehow to make an inroad for respect of metaphysical studies by the scientific community.

After receiving my degree, I was encouraged to pursue a Ph.D. in designing scientific tests to measure metaphysical principles. However, at this point, even after being apparently successful in bringing metaphysics into the university, I began to see the folly of this marriage of metaphysics and science. They have different premises. The method of scientific inquiry leads to designing an experiment that rules out all influences other than those the experimenter is controlling. The premise of metaphysics begins with the interrelatedness of all reality and the impossibility of isolating events within the experimenter's control.

I saw that the scientific, academic part of our mind is limited in its ability to explore the metaphysical aspects of life. Science has its place, but I saw that it has to be set aside if you are to explore your metaphysical realities. Science has no soul. It ignores that which can't be measured or proven—that's *its* filter. Inner world experiences can't be measured or proven, but are experienced every day.

We all have an inner world—don't doubt your experiences just because science can't prove them. Your inner experiences wouldn't stand up in a court of law either. Again, the wrong filter. You must cultivate the mystical side of your character, trust your experiences, be with your true spirit, and not judge yourself by outer standards. No one is a better authority of your relationship to energy than you. This is highly personal, so again, what is written here is not as important as what this evokes within you.

Understanding the chakras is one of the most effective means for accessing the various levels of consciousness available to you. It is a simple system to comprehend and, yet it is profound, as a guide to the inner world. You are already experiencing them. The chakra model gives you a way of identifying the *type* of energy you are experiencing: survival, pleasure/sexuality, power, love, creativity, intuition, and spirituality. Each of these seven levels of energy are animated by the seven chakras.

In this book, I will present the model in its traditional way of understanding and then expand on it. In this way, I will use the chakra model as a template to provide a structure for exploration. But I will also take creative license, based on years of experience, to go far beyond the traditional way of using the chakras. I expect that each reader will have a different reaction, and this is good. I do not present these ideas as absolute truth, instead they are "works in progress," and when the reader has a different experience than I present, I encourage you to go with your personal truth. That is what it is all about: accessing your direct personal experience of the various centers of consciousness.

Give it a try and your direct experience will verify the validity of its merit as a guide for perceiving life's experiences. It helps you to know what level of consciousness you are operating from at any time. It gives you a map for activating and experiencing other levels of consciousness. When problems, challenges, and difficulties arise in your life, the chakra model gives you a tool for helping to identify the source of the conflict within yourself. All seekers on the path eventually realize this: identifying the source within is the key for liberating the self.

The ideal is to become elastic in consciousness: to move freely throughout the totality of your being; to sink fully into the meaning of your personal life and the lessons of this incarnation and still be able to rise up out of your separate self to experience the beauty of your connection to collective issues, and the Divine.

In this exploration of the chakras I will focus on the seven main traditional chakras. There is much speculation these days about chakras beyond the traditional seven becoming available for us. I will, however, set aside this view for this book and focus exclusively on the classical seven.

Section I
Introduction

The Chakras: the Energy of Life

LIFE IS ENERGY, and the chakras are about energy. The universal life force circulates through us and brings us the experience of life. The chakras are the storehouses and transmitters of the universal energy, and each of the chakras represent distinct frequencies within the universal. The chakras interact with the electromagnetic energy field and transform this into the energy that sustains our lives.

The chakras are the conduits through which the universal energy flows. Our personal sense of this is that it moves from the earth through the lower chakras to the upper chakras, but it is not linear—it is cyclic and runs both ways.

Compare this to how photosynthesis works in the plant world. The sun's energy is absorbed by the material substance of the plant and brings it to life. The energy is drawn down into the roots, which draw nutrients from the earth. The energy then ascends back up the plant and is ultimately expressed as its flowering—energy transformed into beauty and given back to the world. So it is with us. We draw in energy from the sun, it is drawn down to the root of our being, draws from the earth, and then it ascends—ultimately becoming the flowering of our being as it is offered back to

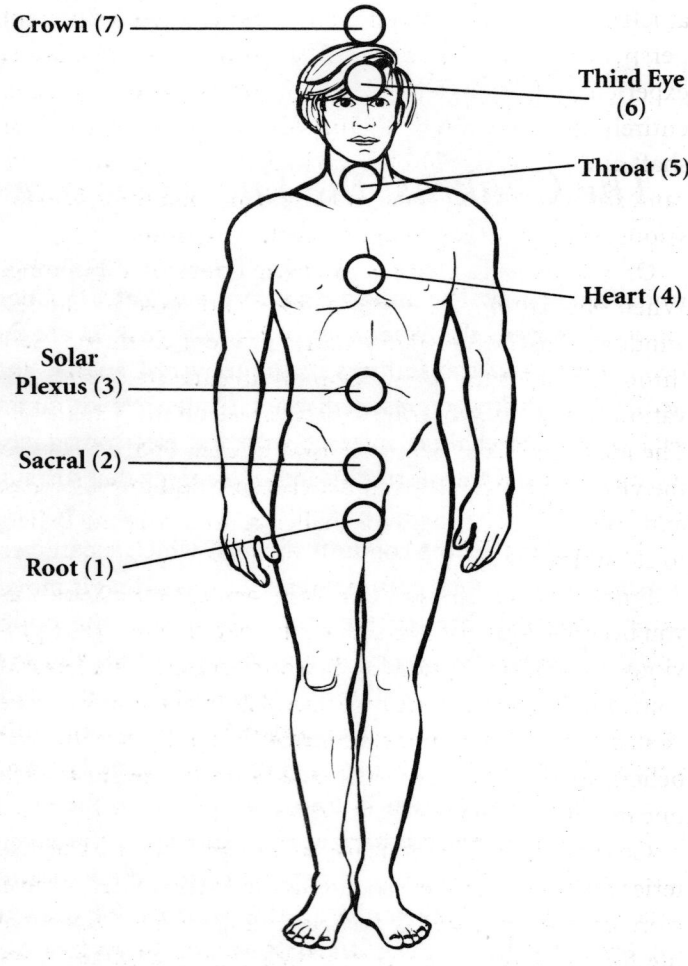

Figure 1: Chakra points on the human body

The Chakras: the Energy of Life

the world. As we work with our consciousness, it becomes more of an expression of beauty.

The chakras are spinning vortexes of subtle energy located along the spine from the base to the crown (see Figure 1, at left). Each of these seven main chakras offers a different perspective on life or any given situation. The same issue, experienced from different levels of consciousness, takes on entirely new meanings. Picture the spine as an elevator shaft and the chakras as the various floors from which we can experience life. When you rise from one floor of consciousness to another, your perspective expands.

Or imagine the chakras as seven floors of a building. When you are on the bottom floor and looking out the window, the view is significantly different from the view through each of the other floors. With each successive elevation, one's view becomes successively more expansive. The ideal is to have clean windows at each of the floors so the view can be the clearest. Beliefs can cloud the windows, and you have to be ready to challenge your existing beliefs to clean them.

From each successive floor, your perception expands as you become aware of a larger reality that includes your previous floor of perception, and also includes a vista beyond your previous perceptual capacity. Clear perception is the goal: clean windows, not clouded by culturally conditioned beliefs. As you consider each chakra, reflect on how each one manifests in your life.

Chakras determine your use of energy. They are the batteries for the various levels of your life energy. They receive, store, and express energy by interacting with the universal life force. The freedom with which energy can flow back and forth between you and the universe is in direct correlation to the total health and well-being you experience.

Any blocks or restrictions to either reception or expression of this life energy will result in a malfunction of the organism as a whole, and will be expressed as disease, discomfort, lack of energy, fear, or an emotional imbalance. By acquainting yourself with the chakra system, how it works and how it should operate optimally, you can perceive your own blocks and restrictions and develop guidelines for relieving entanglements. By blockage, I mean restriction, as complete blockage would result in a disconnection with the universal life force—i.e., physical death.

Everyone has chakras and all of them function. This inclusive statement should relieve those of you who are concerned about whether you have all the chakras or not. If you are alive, you do! It is surprising how many people have been told that all of their chakras aren't operating. They are. The degree of efficiency is the factor that varies between individuals and between different stages in that individual's life.

The first level of understanding the chakras is to see them operating in your life as the flow of energy. The same life force that flows through all of the trees, plants, animals, clouds, rivers and mountains, flows through you. It does so through the system of the chakras in an organized, perceptible manner. This can be observed and experienced, but first one must develop the perspective of the witness.

The gradations of energy that the chakras represent are subtle distinctions of the universal life force. Since observing this distinction requires a point of watching, this first level of understanding requires the development of a "witness consciousness"—"being in the world, but not of the world," the spiritual saying goes. It involves stretching yourself to be in two levels of experiencing simultaneously—being fully present in the experience of the moment, while

The Chakras: the Energy of Life

simultaneously observing the experience from a point of detachment. This is the witness. You can't tell the players without a scorecard and it is the witness that has the scorecard and can identify the players on the field.

Those who are blessed with vision sensitive enough to perceive the chakras describe them as vortexes of energy, spinning much like wheels of light, each radiating its own color. The faster these wheels spin, the more energy they can receive and transmit. In all cases, the energy frequency is the lowest at the Root Chakra and increases when moving toward the Crown Chakra, like musical notes going up the scale, or the colors of the rainbow from red to violet. The combined expression of all these wheels of light makes up your aura—the subtle radiation of light energy from the chakras.

The chakras are often associated with the endocrine gland system. Their placement in the body corresponds with the location of many of these ductless glands and the meaning of each individual chakra is closely connected to the function of the corresponding gland. It would be a mistake, however, to consider this connection in any way physical. Although located along the spine and positioned just in front of it, the chakras are decidedly not physical.

The energy of the chakras, although subtle rather than physical, permeates all aspects of your life. By becoming aware of each of their influences, you move your attention away from the manifest, and toward the energy behind the events, where real change can occur.

Balance

WORKING WITH THE chakras requires balance. It is the all-pervasive requirement to be able to move through the chakra system at will. Without balance you become polarized in the area of your life that is out of balance. This will create situations, scenarios and issues related to the unbalanced chakra. Trying to achieve balance from a point of imbalance doesn't work—you always overcompensate with too much effort causing an imbalance in the other polarity. Back and forth you go, teeter-tottering past the point of balance by trying to achieve it, instead of sinking into it.

Exercise 1

A one-legged yoga posture demonstrates this. The tree posture is easy to describe. Stand tall and erect with your weight equally distributed on both feet. Shift your weight to your left foot so that your right foot bears no weight on it, and you can pick it up. Now bring your right foot up and brace it against the inside thigh of your left leg. Stretch yourself downward and upward simultaneously to avoid throwing your hip out to the left. Let go of your leg and bring your palms together in

Figure 2: Finding balance with the Tree Posture

prayer posture to your chest. Find the point of balance (see Figure 2, at left).

When you first try this posture, you wobble back and forth, trying to achieve the desired state. You use the large muscles in your legs and abdomen to try to align yourself, but you continue to wobble back and forth, beyond the balance point. Eventually you sink into equilibrium. You align with the center point that is already there! You quit trying, and instead, align to the point of balance within. Notice that even as you become skilled in this posture, you are still making minor adjustments with your feet and toes, but they are definitely more subtle than before.

As it is with the body, so it is with the mind and emotions. It is the same process at all levels. Before you have experienced balance, you try to create this equilibrium with effort—as if it wasn't there to begin with! Eventually, you let go of the effort and align to the balance point within. It sounds paradoxical, but until it is understood, no progress can be made. Balance is the way, conflict is the illusion. You must believe that balance exists somewhere and, if you are sensitive to it, you will align with it.

To translate this into everyday awareness would be to place all faith in balance. Knowing that any decisions you make from a point of imbalance will lead to further requirements for adjustments too. Knowing this, you would defer making decisions from an uncentered place, and simply wait for balance to return. Making decisions from a balanced place leads to balanced decisions. It seems almost too easy to be useful, but the simplest truths are often the most profound.

The passageways from one chakra to the other are in the center, the core of the chakras, the point of balance. Believe in your center. Trust that it can always be found.

Of course, you have to know what balance feels like in order to know if you are experiencing it or not. That is the paradox. If you do not know this place of harmony within, you can't know what this centered point feels like; you have no reference point. Fortunately, there is grace in life, and into each of our lives some harmony will fall. If you are paying attention, you will notice how effortlessly this occurs. This is the path of effortless action: Learning to move through life with greater grace and ease as more of your life comes into harmony.

Conflict begins to disappear from your life as your instincts become trained to move out of a reactionary point of view. Your life begins to work with greater ease. Issues will continue to emerge, but you are able to deal with them by making minor adjustments, as with your toes in the yoga posture. Life will continue to unfold in its mysterious way. The unknown will always present new issues, challenging us in a never ending panorama of opportunities to evolve, but once you learn the art of balance, you apply the same skill in each new situation.

Balance brings a refinement to your life. All of your senses are heightened and are able to enjoy the most subtle experiences. It is as though each sense becomes easier to please. Before balance is achieved, the lower chakras are insatiable—you can never get enough sensation to satisfy the needs of the chakra. As you learn to center yourself, your senses become more refined and it becomes easier to experience satisfaction

Balance

at each of the chakras. Life's simple pleasures begin to hold more meaning for you.

Thich Nhat Hanh finishes one of his talks* with the following idea:

There is no way to Happiness, Happiness is the way.
There is no way to Peace, Peace is the way.
There is no way to Enlightenment, Enlightenment is the way.

We could add, "There is no way to balance, balance is the way."

---

* Thich Nhat Hanh, *The Art of Mindful Living;* Sounds True, 1992.

Surrender

It follows from the preceding discussion that you cannot "achieve" a state of balance. You have to sink into it and surrender into the experience. So it is with each of the energies of the chakras. At the First Chakra, you cannot achieve security, you must enter into the feeling that is present. At the Second Chakra, you cannot achieve pleasure, you must enter into the experience of pleasure that is available to you. As it is with survival and pleasure, so it is with power, love, creativity, intuition and spirituality. You have to know the balanced expression of the energy within you and align with it. (See Appendix on page 160–161 for the chart of chakras.)

Exercise 2

Get yourself in a good daydreaming position—this exercise is pure fantasy. Let yourself imagine a situation where you experience perfect tranquillity. Imagine the scenario in your mind's eye. Imagine feeling in harmony with all of life. Now enter into the feeling of this experience in the here and now. Make the emotion a present experience that you feel. You have just experienced the Heart Chakra.

You could do this exercise with each of the chakras and enter into the feelings of security, power or creativity, or any other. By entering into the experience in present time you activate the chakra and are essentially experiencing the energy of the awakened chakra instead of trying to achieve it. We could call this surrendering into the experience. This requires faith and trust such that if you let go of willful behavior in this chakra, you won't lose ground! It takes the faith and belief that harmony does exist. But you first have to believe that it can be found before you can surrender to it.

Cleaning the Windows

EXPERIENCING HARMONY MERELY by aligning with the point of balance goes against our training. We've learned that life is tough—"Life's a bitch and then you die"—a series of never-ending challenges that will eventually wear you down. If you stay ever vigilant and on your toes, you can stay one step ahead of your eventual downfall, but eventually it is going to "get you." Many of us unconsciously hold these beliefs because they were imprinted upon us without our conscious awareness. These unconsciously held beliefs push us toward our lower chakras—the "survival of the fittest" mentality.

Understanding your chakras can help break the yoke that ties you to the cultural beliefs you've assimilated. If you are often unbalanced in a particular chakra, you are likely attempting to maintain an inherently false image of yourself. False, in that it is not genuine to you, and doesn't lead you to your center, but to a state of imbalance. If it led you to your center, you would not experience imbalance.

These false images are incorporated into your self-image when you over-respond and adapt to other people's view of you. What role did you play within your family? Everyone assumes a role within the dynamics of the family, and this early identity of the self within the family is strong conditioning. This will drive you to maintain certain behavior patterns consistent with your family role until you do the work of liberating yourself.

If you were the oldest child, you likely took on the family role as the responsible one. Do you have an over-developed Third Chakra, a difficulty in surrendering control in most situations? Or were you the youngest child, with a tendency to defer to others for your security? This would likely lead to an unbalanced First Chakra and a tendency for dependency on others. Or were you the family troublemaker? Peacemaker? Black Sheep? All these roles condition us to patterns of behavior. If you are consistently unbalanced in a particular chakra, consider your early childhood role within your family and see if some of the roots of your current behavior began there. When you can identify the sources of patterns in your behavior, it is easier to overcome the reactionary behavior and enter into conscious choice of what is in your best interest.

Breaking family ties and cultural imprints, whether they were spoken or unspoken, is essential to know your most genuine self. We do not want to assume that all conditioning was inappropriate; some conditioning may have lead to patterns that are perfectly healthy for you. However, it is likely that some of the imprinting was not supportive of your most natural way of being. It is clear that an over-reaction against this early imprinting would also throw you into imbalance, leading to a tendency to react, rather than respond, to situations, and therefore, not allowing your conscious choice to enter in.

Develop the witness point in consciousness to observe yourself in your life. Know that you are meant to live in harmony, and if this is not your experience, find the patterns.

Cleaning the Windows

Observe yourself and notice the hooks that pull you out of your center. Simply said, you must let go of harmful behaviors that you are holding onto. Essentially, you depersonalize the issues by detaching yourself from them. As the saying goes, to experience harmony, let go of your need to be right.

Let's say you are constantly unbalanced in the Second Chakra with tendencies toward excessive focus on sensory gratification. Could the roots of this be in your early childhood? Were your senses deprived, leaving you with the feeling of never quite getting your fill of pleasure? Was there a lack of affection? Were you not breast fed? Is the insatiable urge for pleasure in your adult life a futile attempt to gain the pleasure you missed as a child?

This is the questioning you want to pursue in tracking down the source of your imbalance. As you observe your behavior and stay conscious of its source simultaneously, it helps you to make conscious choices instead of simply following a blind impulse consistently leading to a state of imbalance. In this example, you would want to focus on the balanced expression of the Second Chakra and attempt to become more aligned with it. This would be the ability to experience pleasure, not simply chase it (see section on the balanced Second Chakra, page 38). This also works well with imbalances in other chakras.

SECTION II
The Chakras

THE FOLLOWING IS a detailed description of each of the chakras in their balanced and unbalanced states. Each chakra will be explored at various levels: the *Drive* of each chakra, that pulls our attention to it; the *Perception,* how life looks through each chakra; the *Unbalanced Expression* caused by awakening to this chakra, but not yet successfully integrating the experiences into your life; *Sustaining Consciousness,* or what it takes to keep this level of consciousness balanced and integrated; the *Purpose* associated with each of the upper chakras. Colors and crystals that help activate each chakra will be suggested, too. Finally we will explore tips on how to integrate each chakra into everyday situations, showing how they can be most useful.

The Urge for Survival:
Your First Chakra

Color: *Red*
Crystals: *Ruby, garnet, obsidian*
Location: *Base of the tailbone*

THIS IS THE root of your being and your deepest connection to your body and earth. Each of us has a body and its animal nature. There is obviously more to us than just our animal nature, but it is a vital part of our total being.

The primary drive associated with this chakra is survival. It is the most instinctive of all the chakras. Food, clothing, shelter and protection are the necessities to which it responds. Sex, for procreation and perpetuation of the species, is also a drive from this chakra. In a word, *survival* is the basic urge.

To understand the First Chakra, pay close attention to your animal nature and what it takes to stay vital. You have a body. The clearest energy comes to you when you find the spot on earth that most enlivens your physical being. Each animal in nature has a different habitat on the planet that it thrives in. What type of environment and habitat most stimulates your being? Ideally, you would walk out your door in the morning and feel invigorated by the climate, the vegetation, and simply the *feel* of the environment.

This is a very individual issue. Some people thrive in the mountains, some on hot beaches, some in perfectly cultivated gardens, some in cities and some in the wide open spaces. Find your connection to this vital life force. This can cause a confrontation with your beliefs. What if your power point on earth is not convenient to the life you have created? Many of us are born to places that do not fit our basic life connection. If this is the case for you, then you may want to explore and find out what environment most enlivens you.

Seek it out one way or another. If you cannot picture yourself moving to a place where you are most naturally charged by nature, seek it out where you live. Nature is ever present, even in the cities. Something is growing somewhere. Participate. Interact with the life force and feel the invigoration. Bring flowers into your home or office. Find a favorite tree that you can form a relationship with. My wife likes to take a morning run and on her route she has found a tree that speaks to her. She named her tree friend and stops on her run to hug and interact with her friend. The human body in each of us needs an interaction with nature in some way. The drive of a healthy First Chakra seeks out this contact.

The Survival Perspective

This chakra is the bottom floor, where the individuation process starts. It takes no effort to perceive from this level; it is built-in as instinct for survival. This is the animal in us, the part of us that is furthest away from divine union and acts with the survival instinct of the jungle: "Trust no one."

This chakra is where the first test in consciousness occurs. This is where you ultimately stand up for your separate sense of self or be swallowed up in the culturally encoded norms of your time. We all receive cultural conditioning, spoken and unspoken. The expectations of family, school, church, friends, and coworkers provide a strong message of how we should be according to others. If you fail to evaluate this conditioning in terms of asking yourself if these influences really work for you, then feeling disconnected to your own life will likely be the result. When you are successful at a life that others would choose for you, but it is not born of your spirit, you will experience drudgery.

You also have to face the test of security here. Will you act with faith or fear about survival issues? This is the test. Fear drives us further into the sense of separation. Faith leads us out of separation and into the awareness of the flow of life that is greater than ourselves. There must be a faith in a greater reality beyond separateness to balance this chakra.

The First Chakra perspective is dominated by survival issues. Either you are balanced or unbalanced here. If balanced, you have sought out and found the environment that your physical being thrives in. Your survival happens naturally and gracefully as you find the way to enjoy developing the skills required for survival. Your life works.

Unbalanced Expression of Survival

The primary clue to a condition of imbalance is a feeling of insecurity. If there are not enough resources to provide adequate food, clothing, or shelter, the needs of this chakra will be so consuming that you will find it very difficult to focus on anything else. One of the challenges of meeting these needs is recognizing they are different for each individual, and you must discover for yourself what you need to feel secure.

If unbalanced, fear of insufficiency has clouded your perceptions, sending you into an insecurity cycle—feeling insecure and approaching life as a victim, you find all too many scenarios that support your view of scarcity. As long as survival issues are in a state of imbalance, you are not free to move into the expanded perspective of the other chakras. Knowing this should motivate you into bringing this First Chakra into balance, allowing you to rise in consciousness.

When the needs of this chakra are not balanced, your perspective will be distorted by the lens of insecurity. All of us are familiar with these feelings. If you have bought into the cultural notion that security is a "defense posture," then you are caught up in constantly trying to fortify your defenses, just in case. Alternately, an imbalance could manifest as an actual lack of abundance in the material world, reflecting and justifying the inner imbalance.

Remember, an energetic view of life always looks to your relationship with the energy of the chakra first, and the manifestation in the world, second. Don't wait for the physical world to come into balance in order for you to feel balance here. It doesn't work. The outer imbalance is a reflection of the inner imbalance. Let's get this straight: The inner imbalance is not caused by situations in the world, the inner imbalance creates situations in the outer world. This is the energetic view of life—change the inner experience of energy and the outer world will follow.

Exercise 3

When feeling insecure because of the unpaid bills, or a possible lack of income, try this exercise for cultivating a non-monetary base of security. First approach your situation from an energy perspective—realize that the outer world is not creating the experience. Of course, from the ego's perspective, it looks exactly as if the insecure feelings are because of the bills. Try to remember this is the illusion that we so easily fall into. To cure yourself of this insecurity, go for a walk in nature. Not to exercise, but to commune. Notice the abundance of life and contemplate the universal life force running through all of nature. There is enough life force to animate all the various plants and trees, the animals, the rivers, clouds, everything. It is the same life force coursing through all of nature. Eventually, feel that same life force moving through you. And then it hits you, you are not just *living life,* life is *living you!* Realize that it is not your will that gets your heart beating, your lungs breathing, or your blood pumping. There is a force greater than you that is animating all of life and you are part of that fabric. Ah . . . all of a sudden, your insecurity has passed.

Many people unbalanced in the First Chakra are attempting to fit into a life that others think is appropriate without sufficient self-analysis to determine if these situations actually meet their true needs. If this is your situation, you will find yourself with a hunger that demands attention.

An obvious example is the young mother with three children whose husband has abandoned them. The pressing needs for survival will be a consuming factor for her energy. A not-so-obvious example is of the young man who was able to succeed in society before he discovered what his own values are. There may be an abundance of food, clothing and shelter available and no apparent reason for his feeling insecure. However, if material wealth is not personally meaningful to him, worldly security will feel empty and he will still hunger for inner security. Perhaps he has acquired a penthouse apartment right in the middle of a big city, because that was the expected thing for a person of his status to do. If this fulfills his personal security needs, then this would be fine. If, however, he is someone who actually needs to live in the country for his well-being, then he will still feel insecure, with the sensation of having no real roots, no matter how plush his penthouse. This is why it is so important to discover one's own needs by honest introspection and self-awareness.

Sustaining a Balanced Survival Level of Consciousness

Your First Chakra consciousness is exclusively physical. Maintaining physical life is all consuming, as survival is the focal point of its consciousness. "Kill or be killed," the law of the jungle, is the modus operandi of the First Chakra. Even with sex, there is no tenderness—it is lust that drives the First Chakra. Sex at this level is just a drive; nothing more than the biological drive to perpetuate the species. From this center, sex feels more like "getting laid" than "making love."

It is easy to dismiss the First Chakra as brutish, but we should remember that if we do not survive, consideration of the other chakras is merely academic! The healthy manifestations of the First Chakra level of consciousness include a sense of safety, knowledge of how to ground one's being, and feeling connected to the body and the planet, and an acute awareness of the instincts that protect the self.

Grounding can be cultivated by any activity that directly connects you to the earth—gardening, hiking and walking barefoot on the earth are chief among these. Grounding can also be facilitated by visualization.

Exercise 4

Imagine a grounding cord that runs from your spine deep into the earth. Imagine in your mind's eye any excessive mental energy running down your spine and dissipating through the grounding cord into earth. Imagine the grounding cord growing roots, like giant trees. Picture the roots of your grounding cord intermingling with the roots of the giant trees. Now imagine that you can draw energy up from the earth through your grounding cord. Picture the same centered strength of the trees being accessible to you, too.

Sports are an obviously healthy way to engage the First Chakra. The more competitive, physical, and the more risk involved, the more it is a First Chakra sport. Boxing and football are prime examples of this rugged, aggressive energy. Skydiving, race car driving, and similar activities where survival risks are high also are First Chakra activities. Thrill-seeking activities such as amusement park rides and any type of sneaking around with the hope of not getting caught also apply!

This chakra is within the deepest, most personal aspect of the self. It is far away from the collective chakras and, thus, is the most defensive, competitive, "I"-oriented of all. When we feel that our survival is threatened, the rules change. Preservation of the self is a strong instinct.

Species memory fuels the instincts here—biological encoding. It is not just an attitude or belief. It is instinct that is the end result of your species evolution; the instinct of survival. If you operate from this level of consciousness, staying alive is your primary objective; just getting by feels like a challenge. Fear, rather than faith, guides your actions.

This is the point in consciousness that experiences the greatest separation from spirit. If you are at this level, it is easy to feel isolated and cut off from the joys of life that others seem to have. Enjoying life seems out of the question when you are totally absorbed in just getting by. You need to get out, into nature, and drop into your animal nature. Feel alive, then the Second Chakra experiences are much more likely to occur for you.

To sustain balance here, your station in life, your home, job and family, must provide adequate resources to meet your basic security needs. Your feelings about this area of life can range from adequacy to abundance, but the main thing is to have no pressing needs. To achieve such a state of balance you must recognize what your needs are in this area and be resourceful enough to provide the proper situations to meet those needs. When the energy is in a state of balance, it naturally rises to the Second Chakra.

Remember, if your focus does not rise above this chakra, the needs of the chakra will appear insatiable. The rich person who has more money than anyone in the bank—and still feels inadequate or insecure—is the perfect example of this situation.

*Tips for Awakening Your **FIRST** Chakra*

THERE ARE MANY situations in life where fear motivates behavior. If you are feeling off-center, check your energy field and notice if insecurities and fears are dominating your consciousness. These are clues to the need of bringing your First Chakra into balance.

Or, if you simply feel a need for greater security, passion, strength and intensity, again focus on the First Chakra. Try doing the tree posture to ground and balance yourself. To

Your First Chakra

activate the power of your instinctual animal nature, go out into nature and feel yourself as being part of the fabric of life. Know that your roots are drawing from the same vital life force as the great trees. Visualize the color red and feel its power and vitality coursing through you. You could wear a red shirt or scarf to support your efforts. Go for a walk with a focus on seeing how many ways you can tune into the color red. Hold onto a garnet, ruby, or obsidian as a touchstone to help you to align with balanced strength and passion.

Fear is meant to function as an alarm, not as a state of consciousness. By knowing how to activate and balance your First Chakra you can disengage from a fear-based mentality. You know that your animal instincts are highly tuned and you picture them as being on alert in the background. If any real danger presents itself (a car about to hit you in the crosswalk), trust that your instincts will sound the appropriate alarm and remove you from harm's way. This liberates your consciousness, and allows you to focus on more enjoyable pursuits—which is the basis of the Second Chakra.

The Pursuit of Pleasure: Your Second Chakra

Color: *Orange*
Crystals: *Carnelian, amber*
Location: *The pelvis area*

THE PRIMARY DRIVE of this center is the search for pleasure. Sensual and sexual activities become a primary concern. To feel attractive and able to draw the things to you that you desire is another need of the Second Chakra, along with desire to lose yourself in the world of sensations. It drives you to feel life fully and awakens the emotional life. Where the First Chakra is satisfied by just surviving, the Second Chakra awakens the desire to enjoy the experience, too.

The Pleasure Perspective

The Second Chakra perspective is animated by magnetism. What attracts you, and what are you repelled by? This arousal of energy most often is dominated by sexuality, but certainly not limited to it. From the experience of fulfillment to the quest for hedonism, to the disappointment of unrequited love, the Second Chakra perspective offers whole new levels to life experience. Beyond survival, the quest of the Second Chakra is to enjoy the experience of life.

Living a life guided by magnetism empowers even the most mundane experiences, and transforms them into something special. It is a path laden with danger, however, because as you awaken to magnetism you eventually realize that it is not just *healthy* experiences that you attract. As your magnetism increases, you also attract greater opportunities to fall off your path! This ultimately leads to the development of personal values. Without values, the search for pleasure reduces itself to hedonism and the undisciplined life. Your values guide you to allow certain pleasurable opportunities into your life, and to develop discrimination regarding opportunities that are not in your best interest.

The benefit of the magnetic perspective is that it feels exhilarating and frees one from the sense of drudgery of a life based on duty. It is energizing to experience life with the spark of the Second Chakra. The wisdom teachings from many cultures suggest that the search for pleasure leads to certain downfall and therefore mandate a path of renunciation and celibacy. It is easy to understand this advice, because it is quite difficult to actually experience the fullness of pleasure this chakra offers and still maintain balance. The skill of learning how to enter into the sensation of enjoyment is required.

To experience pleasure is one thing, but to recognize the experience as enjoyable and then enter into the felt sense of appreciation of the moment—now *that* is an art. There is a hunger in the Second Chakra that can easily become insatiable until you learn how to enter into the experience, and not just the chase, of enjoyment. Looking through the lens of this chakra, you see opportunities to experience pleasure. With a balanced Second Chakra perspective, you take delight in the pleasure of the senses as an integrated aspect of total life.

The Second Chakra grasps for whatever brings pleasure and these experiences habituate very easily. Sex, alcohol, tobacco, chocolate, the sensation of drugs; all are Second Chakra, and all very habit forming. The lure of the habit overcomes the individual trapped in this center, and the thought of pleasure drives one to indulge. When you are in the habit mode of this center, you are attempting to recreate a pleasure remembered from the past. This obviously cannot lead to fulfillment, as it is missing the immediacy of the moment by looking to the past. Quitting any indulgence rarely works. What is pushed down, grows stronger. Taking part in the indulgence, while simultaneously staying aware, is the antidote.

We tend to lose awareness during the pursuit of pleasure. The trick is to stay fully conscious and mindful during the experience. This is quite different than attempting to quit the experience. Quitting something seems like a loss to some part of our character and the yearning for the experience never leaves; it remains pushed down. It is better to simply let your indulgences drop away as they no longer serve you. As you focus more on pleasure, instead of the *pursuit* of pleasure, you will leave certain indulgences behind because of a conscious awareness that the experience no longer leads to the promised pleasure. This awareness obviously is born from being aware during the experience, not pre-experience and not post-experience, but *during* the experience.

Exercise 5

Consider an experience of pleasure gratification that you often take part in, but tend to feel guilty about. Reach for the object of pleasure and experience it with full awareness. How do you experience the sensation of this experience? Is it enjoyable? Where in your body is the enjoyment centered? Bring your full awareness to the experience. You will find that this sensitizes your capacity for pleasure and you are satisfied with less.

I call this exercise "The Chocolate Cake Diet" approach. The next time you are drawn to eating chocolate cake (or any other indulgence), get past your judgments of this and get into the experience. Slow down the whole process to deepen the experience of pleasure. Luxuriate in each bite. Let the flavor roll around in your mouth and be aware of how each taste bud is exploding with ecstasy. Don't gulp past the experience of pleasure, and then see what happens next. You feel complete and full with the experience and you might not have even finished the piece of cake! You gave yourself to the fullness of the experience.

Unbalanced Expression of Pleasure

If unbalanced, the search for pleasure is not completed by a sense of fulfillment and the chase is on. The search for pleasure is never satisfied, so the endless quest for sensation begins. Where balance in this chakra refines your sensitivities to pleasure, imbalance leads to insensitivity and baser values. Stronger and stronger doses of pleasure are required to get through the numbness surrounding the heart. Is it the wounds of previous experiences or the cynical callousness of mistrust that blocks the balanced perspective? Whatever it is, it is not worth it; let go of the issue and come

Your Second Chakra

back into balance by finding something to enjoy and experience with the totality of your being. Ah! Life experienced from a balanced Second Chakra is certainly more enjoyable.

The major clue for noticing an imbalance in the Second Chakra is a desire to lose yourself in sex, drugs, alcohol, food or any stimulating sensations. Consuming sexual fantasies, although not actual activity, are still motivated by the desire of this chakra driving the imagination. This could easily lead to viewing everyone in terms of their sexual potential. Ram Dass once said, "people looking at life through this channel see everyone as either make-able, non-make-able, or irrelevant!"

We attach to our pleasures very easily, and the fear of losing these pleasures leads to an unbalanced perspective from this center. Jealousy and over-attachment are the chief culprits here. Driven by fear of loss, a sense of fulfillment becomes impossible. This does stimulate the Second Chakra in that strong passions are awakened from this imbalance. Life doesn't get any more intense than the experience of good ol' jealous rage! It works to stir deep passionate emotions and, in this way, awakens the Second Chakra. However, it is a destructive emotion and all that results from this state leads to further suffering.

To create balance while in a state of jealous rage is no small trick, but it can be accomplished. Remember, *energy* first, then *manifestation*. The only way to regain balance is from the inside out. You have to get there yourself; not wait for the external situation to change.

When I find myself in a state of jealousy, I first remember that I am in a state of inward imbalance and this is where the work needs to be done. Then, I remember that I am only accountable for how well I live up to my own moral and ethical standards. It is not my responsibility, nor in my power to control, how others live their lives. This line of contemplation always brings my focus back to something I have some control over—me. How am I doing with my ability to live up to my standards?

Another imbalance from the opposite polarity is anxiety concerning your attractiveness. Here, it is especially important to know your true nature, because the marketing techniques of our mass media aim right at this center. Statements such as "unless you use our product, you won't get your man," etc., promote an imbalance by stating that your natural attractiveness is somehow inadequate. Fashion can be both a creative expression and, at times, an anxiety-producing pressure with the Second Chakra. If you feel anxious about your physical appearance and attractiveness, this is a pull from this chakra. If playing with your appearance is fun and enjoyable, by all means this can be a healthy activity. However, if you are constantly feeling unattractive, or have anxiety about being seen unless you are "put together," then it has likely gone too far and you'll need to reconnect with your own inner beauty and attractiveness to regain balance.

You can also feel inadequate or uncomfortable in social situations over your perceived inability to measure up to others. When you compare yourself to others and always come up short, or when you feel envy for what other people have, these are again clues of a lack of balance in the Second Chakra.

Sustaining a Balanced Pleasure Level of Consciousness

You experience a balanced Pleasure Chakra when you have a creative and controlled passion for life. An ability to lose yourself spontaneously in the wonder of life makes delving

Your Second Chakra

into instincts and passions a creative expression. Your sexual life is harmonious with your needs, which makes intimacy an enriching, rather than anxious, area of your life. Involvement with nature, art, dance and beauty of all forms are techniques for enriching this chakra.

When you have awakened to this level of consciousness, your senses come alive and you typically have a strong urge for some type of creative activity. This comes from a deep appreciation for beauty and a desire to bring more of its delight into your life.

Self-assurance is another sure sign of balance, one based on a positive self-image, knowing that you have the ability to attract all that you will need from the universe. It is a God/Goddess-given right, and has little to do with physical beauty. This awareness cultivates an inner sense of attractiveness, and an outer magnetism that reflects it.

Cultivating a balanced Second Chakra requires you to enter into deep satisfaction while experiencing the delight of your senses.

Exercise 6

In the middle of a hug, or while tasting something delightful, listening to beautiful music, or witnessing an exquisite sunset, close your eyes for a moment and focus on the deep sense of satisfaction you are feeling. Along the same lines, after experiencing a sexual embrace with your lover, close your eyes and enter into thankfulness for the experience and focus on the delight of the sensations within your body. Notice that every cell in your body is alive with pleasure. Cultivate that sense of satisfaction. You will find that this leads to an awareness of *fullness* and *completion*.

When the search for pleasure is balanced with the art of experiencing enjoyment, life becomes a delightful experience. For one who has eyes to see it, earth offers a bounty of enjoyable opportunities. This balance leads to a refinement of your sensitivities and enhances your capacity for enjoyment.

A trap of experiencing life from the Second Chakra is how easy it is to become obsessive with sexuality and magnetism. Everyone has magnetism, and the Second Chakra level of consciousness is aware of this flow of energy between people. When unbalanced, it is as if you are "on the prowl," pursuing the next form of pleasure. When integrated, this magnetism adds to the spark of life and makes all interactions with others lively and pleasurable. When balanced, the seductive, hunter/huntress quality of this chakra is dropped and the current of magnetic energy is simply there to add to the enjoyment of the moment.

Desire and appreciation are both of the Second Chakra, but they lead to very different experiences. Desire could be characterized by focusing on what you want, but don't have. Pornography is a prime example of this type of activity, though rather extreme. Focusing on wanting anything is defining yourself in a state of lack. Desire becomes its own reward, as there is a chemical release in the body that can be felt and measured. This release of hormones in the body is not dependent on the completion of the desire; in fact, desire seems to identify with not *having*, but *wanting* the experience.

Appreciation is a higher form of Second Chakra consciousness. Instead of focusing on what you don't have, you learn to take delight in what is available. Here the

Your Second Chakra

consciousness focuses on that which is being experienced and appreciation courses throughout the entire body. This allows for satiation and balance of the Second Chakra. Colors, sunsets, music, hugs and all types of sensory experiences are focused in terms of the satisfaction they bring.

When you're able to sustain consciousness at the second level, you learn to live by the laws of magnetism. You follow energy. You are secure in knowing that life will always be there; it is never a vacuum. The security of knowing that you will always be able to experience pleasure allows greater mobility in your life. You can consider other options, knowing life, with all its delights, will be waiting for you there.

Having options can be both comforting, and distracting. For some, this can lead to an endless awareness of possibilities and various lifestyles that are attractive. Unless you focus on the *fulfillment* aspect of the Second Chakra, you will never be able to fully enjoy life, because you'll always be on the lookout for something better. If balanced with this awareness, you are comforted by knowing you always have other options, but this doesn't distract you from being able to fully enjoy the life you have chosen.

When you have awakened to Second Chakra experiences, but have not yet balanced the First Chakra issues of security, the insecurity gets projected into Second Chakra experiences. Jealousy and envy can result. The Second Chakra drives us to relationships. When you are able to sustain balance at the second level, your capacity to enjoy others for who they are accelerates. Envying others robs you of the ability to enjoy the life you are living. This is disempowering, and as you learn to enjoy others for who they are, these relationships add to who you are.

*Tips for Awakening Your **SECOND** Chakra***

THE NEXT TIME you feel dull, and life seems to have lost its shine, try a conscious immersion in pleasure. For example, you could take a warm bubble bath with candles and your favorite music. Focus on the delight of your senses. Feel every skin cell being caressed by the warm water. Leave your thoughts behind and enter into the music. Open your eyes slightly and notice the candlelight and the dance of light and shadow on the walls. Let go of all guilt and "shoulds" about what you ought to be doing, and fully surrender to the pleasure of the moment. Go to the place within you that notices this pleasure and acknowledge how satisfying it is.

When the magnetism in your relationship has reached low ebb, reinvigorate it with romantic attention. Romance is not just for the bedroom. Remember what it was like when you and your lover were courting. Remember how much effort you put into gaining a smile from your partner. Re-engage the active component of romance; don't simply wish for it, instead, actively pursue it. Create a "date night" on the weekly calendar, a standing date that no matter what else happens that week, the date night never gets ignored. A date weekend once a month or every other month is also great, where the focus is just on the two of you getting away from it all together.

I have a favorite ginseng tea that I can only get it in my home state, so I take it with me when I go out on the road for speaking engagements. Recently, I found that I forgot to pack the tea for one of my trips. I called my wife and asked her to special delivery some to me right away. She did, but also opened up each box and put mailing labels with love notes on each tea bag! Every time I made a cup of tea that

Your Second Chakra

week I also felt her romantic efforts and my heart stayed open to her all week. It is often the "little things" that count.

The next time you are feeling neither magnetic, nor attractive, let go of your focus on physical beauty, and cultivate *inner beauty*. Start the day with a golden chalice meditation:

> Picture, in your mind's eye, your heart like a golden cup—make sure it is upright. Now imagine all the people you have loved and those who have loved you. Picture the warm energy from these images filling your cup. Picture in your mind how many ways you have noticed beauty lately, in nature, a child's laughter, art, wherever. Imagine that the energy of all this beauty is also filling your cup. Imagine the angelic and spiritual levels of life and picture this Divine love coming to you and filling your cup. Then, go out into the world and interact with others. See if you don't feel more magnetic!

The Drive for Power:
Your Third Chakra

Color: *Yellow*
Crystals: *Amber, yellow tourmaline, citrine and topaz*
Location: *The solar plexus*

TO BE SELF-ASSERTIVE and to have a sense of your power, to recognize yourself as an individual separate from the world, and yet able to make an impact on the world, these are the drives of the Third Chakra. From this center, you develop the principles, ethics and beliefs for which you are willing to stand. It also includes the ability to define your boundaries—to say "yes" when you mean yes, and "no" when you mean no. This discernment brings in the intellect, which in turn helps guide the will to those issues it will engage in, and which it will avoid. Your capacity to choose is an important function of the Third Chakra.

The high road from this drive leads to self-mastery in one form of expression or another. This is where self-control, self-restraint and self-discipline come from. However, this is also where petty, or not so petty, power conflicts arise if you haven't developed self-control.

The Power Perspective

Looking at the world through the lens of the Third Chakra, you see opportunities to express your power in the world. This is the seat of your willpower and the center that gives mobility in your life—the ability to initiate activity, to define boundaries, and defend yourself from an encroaching world. Ideally, your perspective gives you free will—the choice to act, or not to act. You awaken to the world of influence, and the perception of willpower being directed at you, or from you.

Through the Third Chakra perspective, you look at life through your sense of what's right and what's wrong. It is where you are asked to stand up for your truth and "show up" for your life. You will get tested in life periodically, and the Third Chakra is where you respond to tests requiring courage. The world of power can seem threatening. Where the First Chakra stands up and defends itself with raw instinct, the Third Chakra's courage must be cultivated. What convictions are you willing to stand for? This is your honor code, on which you must be willing to stake your will.

The intellect is brought into the Third Chakra perspective through *discrimination*. You must know yourself well enough to know what principles are important to you. The right use of will involves discrimination. Not repression, nor denial; discrimination. Knowing how to pick your battles wisely. You want to make sure that you stand up for issues you really do believe in, and not just for the sake of making an issue "because you can."

Where the First Chakra is satisfied by survival, and the Second Chakra is constantly seeking pleasure, the Third

Chakra is about developing self-control. Discernment is the chief characteristic of the healthy Third Chakra, and this is where the mind kicks in. Knowing when enough is enough, when to say no to pleasure, is part of this self-control. It is not just will directed at the world, but also within the self. This is called the discernment of the right use of will.

Unbalanced Expression of Power

Imbalances can come from either polarity: Overuse or underuse of willpower.

Overuse is easy to see. Everything becomes competition. The pecking order gets challenged in every situation, and conflict seems to dominate your life. Everything is a challenge, a test, a battle. At worst, this can lead to ruthless ambition. This imbalance leads to a mistrust of life, a fear of letting go, believing that if you are not in control, things could not possibly go your way. This mistrust of life keeps you on guard, defensive, ready to battle the next challenge.

I call this the "adrenaline junkie" approach to life. When not integrated, the need to prove yourself is so strong that petty power conflicts constantly arise to test you. The conflicts activate the flow of adrenaline and this gives a surge of energy, "a rush." It is quite easy to become an adrenaline addict and thrive on this energy. It is energy all right, but when not balanced, it is not in harmony with the surrounding world and conflict results.

This type of imbalance is particularly hard to break free from, because the adrenaline junkie continually gets into situations of "justifiable anger." The attitude of "I have a right to be mad, look what just happened to me!" is its common territory. In this state, you will continually attract situations that justify— in your mind—the response of anger.

Each of us has a most natural way to be, and when we have aligned with it, conflict stops. An energy approach to life looks at the *energy first* and the *events second*. The person caught in justifiable anger looks at the *events first* and the *energy second*. Events do not cause energy, events are caused by energy, so this approach puts the cart before the horse. It is not until you balance the energy within yourself that the outer world comes into balance.

Clues to under-expression (or underuse) of this chakra are: feeling guilty when you say "no," seeming to invite others to take advantage of you, and acting the "martyr role." Inability to assert yourself and feelings of helplessness are symptoms of this type of imbalance as well. All of these behaviors stem from the lack of self-esteem and self-confidence that the imbalance breeds.

The under-expression of willpower is also easy to see. It is reflected in the frustrated individual who is always having to do things he or she doesn't want to do. If this is you, your life seems to be dominated by the demands of others, rather than following your own heart. Guilt and shame drive you away from standing up for yourself and you seek redemption by being a "good person," and by doing what is expected of you by others.

This type of serving the demands of others is not true service, it is more like being a servant. "Being of service" and being "a servant" may be related, but they are miles apart in how they feel. When you are being of service, helping others feels good. When you are being a servant, the service is expected and demanded of you, and the activity becomes demeaning. This line of distinction between being of service and being a servant is exactly the place that the Third Chakra perspective of defining boundaries can do some good.

The imbalance at the Third Chakra can also stem from imbalances in the first two chakras. If there is insecurity, or an inability to enjoy others, the pecking order game will certainly become your reality. One-upsmanship interferes with your life and you immediately become defensive when confronted with any opposing views. If you are having excessive petty power conflicts, first look to your issues around security and the ability to enjoy other people. If these issues are not in balance, you need to first get at these core issues to establish a balanced foundation—then you can be more effective in working with your Third Chakra power issues.

We will see this principle over and over again as we continue through the chakras—if the energy is not balanced in the lower chakras, the imbalance will interfere with the experiences of the upper chakras. You will have experiences, like flashes of insight, from the upper chakras, but you will not be able to sustain that level of consciousness until the lower chakras are brought into balance.

Sustaining a Balanced Power Level of Consciousness

The ideal is to assert yourself when the situation requires and to have the inner strength to be passive when appropriate. Being able to focus your will to achieve what you want, and to relax your will to enjoy what you have achieved, are qualities of a balanced expression of this chakra. This is the effective use of will—never expressed more than necessary, but always enough to achieve results. A good example is the successful person who succeeds without interfering or challenging others' rights to succeed for themselves.

From a balanced Third Chakra perspective, you are able to feel effective, safe and secure in life. Your self-identity is rooted in a greater awareness of harmony, and you become attentive to your inner process when you feel a lack of balance in your life. You disengage from the outer experience and work directly on your energy to bring it back into balance. You become like a tuning fork and, in interacting with others, you help them return to balance in their lives. Since you are not projecting an imbalance of power, you do not attract power conflicts to you.

This balance gives you flexibility, and you enlist cooperation, rather than competition, from others. Your willpower is effective in that you know when to be decisive when a situation calls for action and input. You are secure enough in your life so that when things are going along smoothly, you can ease off your will and stay in harmony. Your life is mobile and flexible, and you are able to accomplish a great deal because you are not in constant conflict with those around you.

"To experience more peace in your life, give up the need to be right," hits the mark in describing a balanced Third Chakra. However, let's not confuse the Solar Chakra with being passive. It is the power center, and when balanced, power can be used in ways that benefit all, and yet, takes advantage of no one.

As you grow in your ability to use power, there will be inevitable confrontations with those seeking power struggles. As you awaken to the Third Chakra, you can be a "walking fight" waiting to happen! Power seeks power and as your power awakens, you attract those who are working with their power.

Discriminating use of will can be seen in the famed television show *Gunsmoke*. Matt Dillon was a powerful man; he was the sheriff, the "big gun" in town. Each week, some young buck would come into town and want to do battle with him. Matt Dillon had to assess each of these situations as to whether it was really his battle or not. He didn't gun down every young punk that challenged him. He used discernment as the right use of will. If it wasn't his issue, he disappeared from the conflict. It wasn't as if he backed down; he essentially disengaged from the issue. However, if it was an important issue, he stood his ground and entered into the battle.

Exercise 7

You could apply this attitude in your life by asking yourself two important questions the next time you are in a power conflict:

1. Are you *really* threatened? (Is survival or your security really at stake?)
2. Do you really *care* about the *outcome*? (If you win the battle, does it really matter to you?)

These two important questions will help identify if it is really your issue or not. If your security is not really threatened, or you really don't care about the outcome, it is not your issue. The ego jumps in and says honor is at stake—you've been challenged and you need to defend yourself. This is where you have to know that it is really not your issue. Then you need to use your willpower to avoid the situation. Otherwise you become a scratching post for others to sharpen their claws on. They are testing their power on you, and you are submitting to this by getting involved with an issue that is not your own.

However, if the answer is yes to either of the questions, you *are* either threatened or you *do* care about the outcome, then fight the battle honorably with the intent to win. Align your intellect with your will by discerning which use of will the current situation demands: your involvement or non-involvement.

The level of consciousness the Third Chakra offers is a sense of personal power and effectiveness in the world. Willpower is demonstrated by the individual at this level. Although physical exertion of energy might be involved, this is not the type of physical energy of the First Chakra, instead it is characterized by the discerning mind being equally involved.

The assertion of will is the main characteristic of this type of consciousness. From the negative examples of constantly engaging power conflicts, to the positive examples of "stick-to-it" dedication, the third level of consciousness is about personal power and standing up for what you believe in.

Where Second Chakra experiences come to you through sheer magnetism, and you can know what you like and don't like, there still isn't the will to say yes or no, with some discernment, until the Third Chakra is awakened. This is the defining chakra. What principles do you stand for? Where are the roots of integrity to your being? This is where your character is formed by standing up for and defending the values you became aware of with the awakening of the Second Chakra.

Great clarity comes into your life when you are able to sustain Third Chakra consciousness. Your ability to stay clear with your intentions keeps confusion to a minimum. Defenses are dropped. You become so clear in your resolve that you are not threatened by opposing views. You are able to be effective in the world without being abrasive.

When you sustain balance in the Third Chakra, it is not unlikely that you quit thinking about power issues altogether. A natural refinement occurs and you are aware of "intent" as the energy of the Third Chakra. Intentions are everything. When power struggles erupt, you immediately check your own intentions, instead of questioning the motivations of others. You have found an honorable path for expressing your power. Honor includes your best interest and the best interest of others as well. You have learned how to never settle for less than your best interest, nor demand more.

Diplomacy becomes natural for you. You can defend yourself when necessary, yet you are not defensive. Since other views are not seen as threatening, no struggle or conflict arises. You have accepted the paradoxical nature of reality—there are as many different views of reality as there are people, each view supported by the various experiences that led to it. You are also effective in initiating the activities that you want to take part in. Since you are not carrying a big defensive charge, you enlist *cooperation,* instead of *competition,* from others.

Tips for Awakening Your **THIRD** Chakra

DRAW ON THE power of your Third Chakra when you need to be decisive. When you are in one of your quandaries of indecision, focus on activating and balancing the Third Chakra. Then trust in what is born from that balance, make your decision, and don't look back.

This is a great center to focus on when you need that little extra push. This allows you to focus your energy. Keeping your attention centered in the Third Chakra during physical exercise helps you to will yourself self to do it—running, swimming, practicing yoga, or lifting weights—the will to do ten laps instead of two, a hundred situps instead of fifty. It activates your "second wind."

Use the Third Chakra for resolving conflicts (court or otherwise), expressing yourself clearly, taking tests, centering yourself when you get pulled over for speeding and you have to talk to the traffic cop. Breathe deep into your solar plexus and center yourself. Move away from reactions, drop into your center—then proceed.

When you need to pull your mind out of mental "tape loops," use the power of the Third Chakra to will yourself not to indulge in them. Tape loops are those mental patterns that don't lead toward resolution. They just repeat themselves, over and over again, draining your energy, and taking you right back to the start. It takes *focused intent*—exactly the energy of this chakra—to will yourself not to engage these pointless uses of your energy.

When you feel overwhelmed and you have no self-control, activate your Third Chakra. Feeling overwhelmed always stems from the illusion that everything is happening at once. In truth, it is always just one moment at a time: you are just here and now in this moment. On the most overwhelming days, ask yourself, "If I only had the one thing in front of me to do today, would I still feel overwhelmed?" Most often, you'll find that, no, you wouldn't feel overwhelmed if it was just the one thing in front of you. Get there. And do each of the series of "one things" throughout the day with the same attitude. Now you've put your Third Chakra to good use!

The Quest for Love:
Your Fourth Chakra

Color: *Green (Pink)*
Crystals: *Aventurine, rose quartz*
Location: *The heart*

WHEN WE TALK in our spiritual circles about awakening to the "path of the heart," we refer to this wellspring of creation: Love. The path of the heart is one that springs from your being with warmth and joy. It is not strategic, like a good plan, or anything similar. It comes from the place within each of us that is joyful. It is trusting that if you live your life from this place of consciousness, all will work out in the material world as well.

It takes faith, because the modern view of life is one of *struggle,* and its insistence that you had better have a good plan to defend, protect and provide for yourself. This comes from a fear-based mentality—fear of scarcity. The path of the heart gives no harbor to this fear. You must have faith that you will draw to yourself a bountiful life by simply being in that place of magnetic attraction—you *believe* in abundance, and you *attract* abundance.

The more you love, the more you attract experiences into your life to love. It's that simple. Perhaps too simple for us moderns—we are suspicious of anything too simple or free. "You get what you pay for" is an attitude that robs us of some of life's simple and free truths. The awakened heart is one of life's grandest simple truths. It doesn't cost anything or require any sacrifice, but it does take a leap of faith to experience it. You must have faith that you won't get squashed by life for letting down your defenses. And that is exactly what it takes—letting down your defenses to allow life to more freely flow through you. And faith that, indeed, love is the strongest force in the universe.

We are born into separateness. At birth we gain a body, a mind, a personality, and an ego. These define us as separate and unique from all others. The first three chakras deal with the preservation of that separate identity. With the awakening of the fourth, we rise up out of that separateness and begin to experience unity with all life.

The aim of this chakra is to experience love, personal and non-personal. And if not love, at least a harmonious connection that transcends differences between you and others must be felt to satisfy the Heart Chakra. It is through this Fourth Chakra that you begin to merge with collective levels of reality. The lower three chakras deal with individual energy, separate and distinct from all others. The upper three chakras are the collective aspects of the self, increasing the connection with the universal energy. The Heart Chakra is where these two aspects of self meet and merge.

With an awakened heart, you are able to relate to both your personal life and your spiritual life. You are integrated. The heart is the mediator between ego and spirit. You are able to experience the vitality of the lower, physical chakras, as well as the bliss and creativity of the upper chakras. An integrated Heart Chakra is balanced horizontally and vertically. This is your true center, the seat of your soul.

The quest for love goes right to the heart of humanity. Experiencing love—both expressing and receiving—is a core drive within all of us. Finding out what you love to do and doing it, and then sharing the resultant joy with others shows true heart. You are able to accept those you meet and genuinely care for them, without getting drawn into their dramas. Being able to give without thought of what you will receive in return, as well as being able to receive graciously from others, is a conclusive sign of an awakened heart.

Love is the natural outpouring of the heart. Like a mother's love for her child, this is the love that is absolutely selfless—there is no ulterior motive other than love itself. When you love others in such a way that their happiness becomes a high priority in your life, this is the stirring of the Heart Chakra.

The Perspective of Love

The first awakenings of the Heart Chakra perspective are experienced as acts of grace in those rare, fleeting moments when you feel at peace with yourself and the world. Everything is in balance and, seemingly, you haven't a care in the world. You begin to enjoy your own company and with the lower chakras balanced, your ability to enjoy life's simple pleasures is enhanced. This state of being is at first a tease giving you a glimpse of a world beyond survival and competition. As you learn to spend more time in your heart, this becomes a way of life.

From this perspective, you see yourself reflected in everyone you meet. You naturally drop defenses and the competitive way of living life. The heart wants to cooperate, not coerce. The need to be right pulls you back into the lower chakras of competitive views. At the Fourth Chakra, there is nothing to defend, and joy comes from an immense acceptance of life and other people. As the sage Osho said, "Joy is a function of immense acceptance."

The shift from the Third Chakra perspective to the Fourth Chakra is huge since it represents an entire paradigm shift. The sense of rivalry with others is abandoned with the Fourth Chakra as you become aware of dealing with others from the heart. From this perspective, cooperation is the way to get needs met. The sense of abundance accompanies this perspective and you realize there is enough of everything for everyone. Compassion awakens as you see that everyone's best interest is in everyone else's best interest as well. We are all here together; interconnected.

A tremendous sense of calm and tranquillity accompanies looking at the world through the heart. From this vantage point, harmony is the norm, not the rarity that it was previously. Now, when disharmony occurs within the first three chakras, it is easy to make the adjustments to bring your life back into equilibrium, because you are aligned with your path! You know that a centered life is a much greater joy than an uncentered life, and knowing this motivates you to bring your issues back into balance. You become less attached to issues that seemingly bring you out of balance, and more attached to the experience of joy itself. As always, events follow energy, so when you spend more time in harmony, you attract harmonious situations to you as well.

Joy is the natural consequence of looking at life through the Fourth Chakra lens. Since you emanate a calm and joyful presence, you seem to bring out this quality in others, and

Your Fourth Chakra

more people are attracted to you. The more you continue to draw from the universal source, the more people want to spend time with you, and the more you have to give as you pull the universal energy through you and send it to others.

If you forget to draw on the spiritual source, you will start giving too much of yourself and burnout will soon follow. This exhaustion comes from doing it all yourself—you've got the first three chakras balanced, and you are still exhausted. You've awakened to the heart, but forsaken the source. The source is inexhaustible, but you are not. When you are in right alignment, you will be replenished as you give to others of your fullness. When you feel exhaustion, go out into nature and drink in beauty—draw the beauty into you and feel it. Remember, if you are going to give, you need to know how to replenish yourself. The personal is limited, the universal is not. What inspires you? Go and reconnect with your source.

It is a common story. Two people fall in love. Before they were in love, both had cultivated a connection to the source of their inspiration. With their growing love, they spend more and more time drawing from the energy of each other, and less time connecting with their source. Instead of being fully animated by life—in and of itself—and then sharing that with their partner, they depend on each other as the source of their vitality. They become a subtle drain to each other, constantly drawing from the other without replenishing the source.

Imagine a friend that needed five dollars every time he saw you. "Can I borrow $5?" "I'm short $5, can you cover me?" "Do you have an extra $5?" Wouldn't you eventually tire of this friendship, because of it constantly being a drain? So it is in love when you identify the other person as the source of your needs—you become a drain on that person. Remember to stay connected to the sources that inspire you so that you are sharing something vital in the relationship.

With an awakened Fourth Chakra, you look at the world through the lens of love. Love from the first three chakras has need attached to it—there is always an ulterior motive, be it security, sex, or power. But love from the Fourth Chakra is just love for the sake of love itself. It is not attached to needs; you don't need anything from this perspective. You feel fulfilled and are all too willing to share with others. Jesus and the Beatles said it best when they said, "All you need is Love!"

Interpersonal relationships from the Heart Chakra are significantly different than from the first three chakras. Unconditional love is shared with those in your life from the awakened heart. From the first three chakras, it is impossible to see others for who they really are, because you are more focused on how they feed your needs. At the Heart Chakra, love is experienced in a truly non-conditional way. You do not weigh how others fit into your life, instead, you truly enjoy your friends for who they are, in and of themselves. Obviously there will be much greater peace and harmony in Fourth Chakra relationships by you having learned to drop your judgmental attitudes and defensive reactions to others.

Lovemaking changes significantly with the awakened heart. Sex from the lower chakras is need-based—the need for release of pent-up energy, the need for the sensations of pleasure, the need for the feelings of power. Sex from the Fourth Chakra is an absolute blending of giving and receiving. It opens the door for higher-level intimacy, where you learn how to make love with the Divine *and* your partner at the same time. Beyond a purely physical exchange, you make love with your partner at the physical, emotional, mental and spiritual levels.

Unbalanced Expression of Love

Sentimentality is the main component of an unbalanced Fourth Chakra. The "bleeding heart" is unable to separate her problems from those of others. Thus her connection with others is unhealthy and painful. Doing things for others as the price for being accepted is the common result of this imbalance.

Over-attachment in love and codependency are examples of imbalances when the needs for security of the lower chakras interfere with the natural expression of love. Love becomes need and loses much of its shine. "I love you" is being said, but "I need you" is what is meant. This can never lead to balance, because the needs of the lower chakras will worm their way into the Fourth Chakra connection. This leads to love with many strings attached. It is awakened at the heart, but clouded by lower chakra imbalances. These attachments don't allow for the freedom that true Fourth Chakra love is all about.

Exercise 8

If you feel insecure about the object of your love, realize that your issues are about security, not love. Go to the source of the problem. Deal with your insecurities at the First Chakra level. Go for a walk in nature and notice the inexhaustible life force all around you. Feel that same life force moving through you, too. Notice that *you* are not just living life, *life is living you!* Now that you have established this feeling of security with yourself and life, you can enter a relationship fully with that feeling, rather than looking for security within the relationship.

The other difficulty typically experienced with the awakened heart is inappropriate giving. You awaken to the generosity of the Heart Chakra and all too willingly give to others, but are awkward in receiving generosity from others. This is often a product of the moral training, "It is better to give than receive."

Put yourself in the shoes of the people you are gracefully declining when they offer generosity to you, whether it's a compliment, offer for assistance, return favor, or other gift. What is their experience when you decline their offer, no matter what your intent? They feel unappreciated. This diminishes the joy of the moment and is clearly not the Fourth Chakra at its best. Being graciously receptive to the generosity of others is a type of giving—giving to others the joy of pleasing you.

Unconditional love can easily lead to indiscriminate love and believing in qualities of others that simply aren't there; such as falling in love with what you *wish* was true about the other person, or what is *potentially* true. The heart can distort perceptions so that you see more of the good in others. How can this ever be a problem? It is a problem when your perception is so distorted that you can't see the reality in front of you. The awakened heart sees the spiritual potential in all, but forgets that we are all budding Buddhas. The question of "when might this happen?" should enter in when you become enchanted by another's potential.

Restoring balance calls for honest assessment. Ask yourself: do you love the things this person has brought into his life through his own efforts, or do you love this person for who he will be *after* he changes? If it is the latter, this is going to be a project, because you will have to be constantly pumping your life force into this person to realize *your* vision of *his* potential. The problem arises when this is not his view of himself. This type of relationship cannot be sustained, because you will eventually tire of pumping your life force into him. He can't sustain the growth he has obtained through your will, because it wasn't his will that was doing the work. Not surprisingly, he slides back to his old habits. Your vision of his potential might have helped him awaken to his own vision, but ultimately he won't be able to sustain your image of him if it is different from his own.

If you are unbalanced in the Fourth Chakra, you typically can't bear the thought of hurting another person and you avoid anything unpleasant as if it were the plague. By giving into demands of others just to avoid conflict, this allows others to play on your sympathies, and you essentially reward behaviors in others that you don't support.

It would be a mistake to think of the Heart Chakra perspective as all love and light. The soulful qualities of compassion also awaken a deep sensitivity to the sufferings in the world. If not balanced, this empathy can lead to endless grief. Guilt and shame are familiar experiences for the person unbalanced in the Heart Chakra. If you suffer because of the suffering of others, that is only *increasing* the amount of suffering in the world. The failing is in taking the suffering personally, as if it were your fault. This is clearly a personal attachment, which is the domain of the lower chakras. Suffering is part of our journey here; it enters into every life, but ideally you learn how to not attach to the suffering, you give up clinging to the experience and it passes. The heart still breaks as you are touched by the sufferings in the world, but it heals as you move through the experience and on into new life.

If you find yourself unbalanced in this way, go back to the first three chakras and check your alignment there. Are you in vital rapport with your animal nature and have you found the right environment to live in (First Chakra)? Are you able to fully enjoy life by bringing the sense of fulfillment into your pleasurable experiences (Second Chakra)? Are you courageous enough to stand on the principles you believe in (Third Chakra)?

Sustaining a Balanced Love Level of Consciousness

Keeping a balanced perspective from the Heart Chakra is a full-time task. It is very easy to get knocked off the raft of the heart and find yourself struggling in the ocean of emotion. It often happens. The more time you spend on the raft of the heart, the less frequent the tests that knock you off, and you shorten the amount of time that it requires to get back on when you *do* fall off. Just knowing the raft is there gives you motivation to let go of the struggles and turn your attention to the activities and awareness that get you back on board. Always remember that love is the strongest force in the world.

The reward is great. Once you've been able to live from the Heart Chakra, your life changes significantly with evidence of joy and kindness everywhere. You free yourself from the "struggle level" of life that is so evident from the first three chakras. You share the same world, but not the same struggles of others. Tests and difficulties arise as in every life, but with an awakened heart, these challenges are handled with a touch of grace—they are dealt with at the subtlest of levels and life goes on.

When balanced, the soulful perspective fills your life with great meaning. Your compassion for the suffering in the world translates into action, and you do what you can do to alleviate the pain in others. Instead of pulling you down, your compassion pushes you into action.

Your Fourth Chakra

As said before, the leap from the Third Chakra to the Fourth Chakra is huge. A whole different way of viewing life is required—all feelings of separateness drop. A wonderful feeling comes over you: of being here with others experiencing this same miracle of life. This paradigm shift changes your whole view of life, and particularly your way of relating to others.

The consciousness of love can be experienced at three different levels: personal, compassionate, and universal.

Personal Love: At the personal level, the awakened heart takes tremendous delight in the love of the people closest to you. It is true love from an awakened heart that experiences joy with those you love. Romance is one of the most enjoyable aspects of personal love . . . and not just bedroom romance. This is the joy of courtship, like when a relationship is just beginning and you think of all types of ways to bring a smile to your sweetheart. With your Heart Chakra open, you want this type of love forever! If your heart leaps with anticipation as someone you love comes up the walk, you've done a good job with keeping this center vital and open.

This can be cultivated. It happens naturally at the beginning of new love, your heart naturally reaches out to court a response from your beloved. To maintain this romantic energy, maintain the activities of courtship. If you have a family, a date night once a week with your partner is essential. Love notes in the sandwich, special gifts, romantic dinners . . . you remember. Romance is a bit of a game and you have to play the game in order to have the experience on a continuing basis. It's funny how easy and natural this is with young love, but to maintain this requires a skill that must be cultivated, or love soon cools down to "mature" love.

Attachment is still strong at the personal level, because it is still bonded with the first three levels of personal experience. This is often accompanied with the fear of losing your partner. As you awaken to the next level of Compassionate Love, this fear of losing those you love diminishes, finally to be dissolved with the awakening to Universal Love.

Compassionate Love: This level of the awakened heart pulls you out of purely personal love. Compassion can be felt for those that are closest to you, or those you have never met. This is not a personal, possessive love—it has nothing to do with the self. It is impersonal and expansive as you awaken to the soul of the planet and experience this love permeating all of existence. Compassion arises—born out of the awareness that suffering in life results from the feeling of separation, the perspective of the first three chakras.

The Compassionate Heart feels the beauty of each soul struggling to become more conscious. It doesn't have judgment of those who have not awakened beyond the first three chakras; instead, kindness is born. With compassion, you want to help those who are suffering to open to the experience of joy the awakened heart brings.

Forgiveness is perhaps the greatest attribute of the heart awakened to Compassionate Love. It takes compassion to realize that everyone owns a piece of the darkness that shrouds the human experience. We all have drives that are less-than-honorable, and knowing this, you don't hold yourself or others to past mistakes. It's part of the human experience.

However, it is not all roses with the compassion of the Fourth Chakra. When first awakening to suffering, it is easy to become preoccupied with it, and become immobilized. Obviously, this is excessive, and unhealthy. The Fourth Chakra is not about sacrifice; the self has to be full in order to rise up to the heart. The first three chakras must stay balanced in order to maintain Compassionate Love without getting pulled out of the heart.

If you get pulled down into the suffering, you have just added to the amount of suffering in the world, not diminished it. The high road to the compassionate heart does not attach to the suffering. Knowing that the work you are doing on yourself adds as much well being to the planet as any other activity, you return to the work of pulling yourself out of the pain as a compassionate act. When you are anchored in your heart, you are blessed with divine protection—you can touch the suffering of others with a quality of grace felt by everyone.

Universal Love: This is the awakening into the experience of heaven on earth. The first three chakras of earth (Yin energy) and the top three chakras of heaven (Yang energy) merge in the Fourth Chakra of the heart and there is a spontaneous outpouring of love. This is non-attached, non-possessive love and leads to what is commonly called "unconditional love." When mystics tell us that it is love itself coursing through the veins of all reality, we know they are speaking about this aspect of the awakened heart.

When you are able to sustain Heart Chakra consciousness, you abide in a sea of love. Others are drawn to you and you freely give of your spirit. As you give to others, you feel the sensation of the universal energy *flowing through you,* and that is exactly what is happening. Your source of energy is inexhaustible at this level, so you never experience burnout or feel drained by others. Of course, you still feel tired at the end of the day, but not exhausted. You realize that when you experience an energy drain, you are giving from the wrong place. At the first sign of any exhaustion, you know that you have dropped out of the Heart Chakra and into the personal levels. You read the signs in your energy field and reconnect with your sources; then, replenished, you are ready to give to others again.

It is a sweet awakening indeed when you have balanced the heart and integrated its perspective with all of life. All concepts of scarcity dissolve with the awakening to the "abundance of life" perspective that Universal Love brings. This allows you to be gracious and generous with the bounty that life provides. This level of love demonstrates the saying, "Seek ye first the kingdom of heaven inside yourself, and all things will be added upon you."

All attachments drop at the universal level of love. Attachments are fed by fear, and when you are awakened to Universal Love, you refuse to be held hostage by fear. It is not that fear is gone; fear is part of human consciousness—it doesn't just go away. But you can learn to not attend to it. The way is to essentially go away from the fear; realize that fear is a place within you, but there are other places. Understand that fear and faith are essentially flip sides of the same coin—you can experience one or the other. Learn how to withdraw attention from that which leads to fear, and direct attention to that which *empowers your faith*.

Attention is an all important key here. What are you paying attention to? Cultivate a love for life and creation itself, and watch how this reinvestment of your time adds to your life in all ways.

The Soul's Purpose at the Fourth Chakra

Awakening to the energies of the collective chakras always carries with it a responsibility. This comes with the territory and, when fully realized, is gladly performed. Those who are able to sustain their consciousness in the upper chakras never question what their life purpose is—they know. It is a

Your Fourth Chakra

felt sense that is encoded with the experience of the upper chakras. When you awaken to your Heart Chakra, you naturally seek to help others in awakening to the experience of love. You direct people's attention to beauty and love. People feel at peace around you, as no judgment exists within you. This allows others to drop into their true nature in your presence. You create a safe and supportive environment.

You also inspire compassion in others. Your heart is open to all. This openness stimulates others to move beyond their judgments and you feel a sense of purpose when seeing others open up to the love vibration and compassion within their own hearts. This is fulfilled by constantly living life from the awakened Heart Chakra. This "faith in action" that others observe in your life awakens their own faith to live life from the heart.

*Tips for Awakening Your **FOURTH** Chakra*

WHEN YOU FIND yourself feeling exhaustion from being around others, open up your heart. The benefit is great. When you have resistance to another, it is a double-whammy on your energy field. One, you don't get the benefit of energy that comes from receiving, and two, it takes energy to resist. Focus on your heart, drop your defenses, and feel the vitality returning to you.

Any time you try to resolve a conflict with someone else, this is the chakra to focus on. First do the homework by yourself. Count your blessings, enter into thankfulness; this always stirs the heart. Once you are centered and feel the wellspring of warmth, bring your friend's image into this feeling. Feel compassion by realizing here in front of you is another soul struggling with the hardships of existence.

Focus on the heart connection between the two of you. See your upcoming meeting with this person leading right to this place of the heart. Then go do it.

Ram Dass gives the advice of "never place another person out of your heart." He suggests this as a creed for all social action. You may have to discipline another, or express disappointment, or even anger, but never place the person out of your heart. But there is a catch to his great advice—you have to stay *in* your heart to never put the other person out of your heart!

The Voice of Creative Expression:
Your Fifth Chakra

Color: *Sky blue*
Crystals: *Celestite, aquamarine and crysocola*
Location: *The throat*

AS YOU OPEN to your Fifth Chakra, you increasingly learn to accept your originality, whatever form of expression that might take. Not everyone is going to be an artist, but everyone can awaken to creativity and benefit from its expression. Whether it be in the fine arts, or your career, or how you raise your family, creativity is available for everyone. The first step of owning your authentic nature can be a tumultuous ride until you learn to detach from others' view of who you are. Awakening to this dimension begins with self-acceptance of your uniqueness.

The core need of the Throat Chakra is to find your voice and speak your truth. This is not your physical voice, but the place within you from which you speak. To find your authentic voice, be willing to question everything you previously believed. You may end up assimilating much of what you previously knew to be true, but it must first come through a deep process of questioning to establish its validity. When this deep questioning does not first occur, it may feel like you are coming from a liberated point of view, but in truth, you are simply proselytizing your own opinion.

The Fifth Chakra is dominated by the higher mental faculties that allow detachment, observation, and ultimately synthesizing varying views on life. By experimenting with these diverse beliefs, you become aware of their impact on your personal experience. Becoming familiar with different religions and cultural views allows you to creatively impact your life by consciously modifying and expanding your beliefs. This leads to the drive to know and express your own unique truth.

The Fifth Chakra impels you to express yourself in a creative way. This is creativity at the higher-mind level. As personal insights merge and interact with the collective mind, creativity is born. We think of the throat and of speaking, but *self-expression* is more to the point because this level of creativity is certainly not limited to the spoken word. Writing, painting, dancing, music, thinking and countless other forms of creative expression become available to this chakra.

There is a quickening of energy experienced with the opening of the Fifth Chakra. This is first felt as a type of nervousness, a free-floating anxiety that has you feeling jittery and questioning your life. Many people who have stumbled into their Fifth Chakra, without proper preparation and grounding, suffer anxiety attacks, nervous tics, or feeling out of control with the energy. Knowing that the energy is beyond control is the key to aligning with it.

Let's use the image of a surfer riding the biggest wave of his life. He hasn't a hope of quieting down this wave. He can either rise up on top of it and ride it, or get knocked "assover-tea-kettles" up onto the beach—but he can't quiet the wave. So it is with the Fifth Chakra wave of energy—you haven't a hope of quieting the wave. It just *is what it is*—any attempt to calm the energy will ultimately fall short. The way is to *ride the wave*. Breathe deep into the energy and feel yourself rising up on top of the wave and riding it.

Information is encoded within the energy, and if you can handle the wave, incredible "flashes" of information jump into your mind. Your individual intelligence is merging with the collective mind—the womb of creativity. When you merge with the collective mind, magical insights often appear, and you begin to know things you couldn't begin to possibly know. This is the moment of creativity—when insights are born fresh out of the moment. This is where you can court the Muses and feel the touch of their inspiration.

That creativity is born out of the collective is evidenced by noticing how many creative ideas you have had and not acted on. How many times have you seen your ideas acted on by someone else? Go ahead and *don't* write that book you've been inspired to write. You will be able to read it next year, written by someone else. Right?

Since the Fifth Chakra is located in the throat, it follows that you must learn to speak your personal truth, as well as know it. It takes courage to voice an unpopular point of view, but this is certainly the result of an awakened Throat Chakra. You are dealing with this center when you are with a group of friends in a lively discussion and you have an idea, and are trying to decide whether to voice your opinion or not. When this center is integrated, you quit questioning the worth of your opinion (read: lower chakra personal attachments) and join in the group mind by expressing the ideas that come to you.

When I present seminars, I ask people to speak up when ideas come to them. I court the group mind in these presentations and take delight when fresh insights come from the audience. It always amazes me that after the talk someone will invariably come up and mention an idea that she had during the talk. She didn't share the thought at the magic moment, but she wanted to let me know what she was thinking. The unexpressed idea is often a piece that was missing during the discussion, and would have been so helpful in that moment, but offered after the fact, it is more like an editorial comment rather than a contribution.

Knowing yourself at the Fifth Chakra is significantly different than knowing yourself at the Third Chakra. The Third Chakra is about self-control, strategic self-knowledge that, when combined with the personal will, molds the way in which you assert yourself. Self-knowledge at the Fifth level is knowing your tendencies and traits well enough to get out of the way and allow the liberated, pure mind to shine though. It's required you trust that honoring this voice will be in your best interest. Without this faith, you attempt to control this incoming information along lines of your perceived best interest, and immediately it becomes a Third Chakra event.

The Creative Perspective

The rise to the Fifth Chakra is another quantum leap in consciousness. This is the first of the upper chakras and the merging of individual consciousness with the universal. The Fifth Chakra perspective allows the ability for innovative thinking—looking at life with a fresh perspective of discovery, rather than "canned" knowledge. From this perspective, you are not a "capitalist," nor a "communist," nor any other "–ist." You choose to make all decisions based on your independent perspective.

By putting together an unique world view, you challenge others to do the same. People's canned thoughts are boring to you—you challenge others to reconsider their point of view in the moment.

Your independent worldview allows you to look at the world's great religions and philosophies beyond your cultural allegiance. You start becoming a universalist, able to see the beauty in all religions and cultural expressions. Since you have no point of view to defend, you are not threatened by opposing views and are able to stay open to many paths and walks of life.

Having razor-sharp perception, combined with exposure to many belief systems, gives you keen insights. You become a conduit for the universal mind. This allows you to get to the core of issues rather than poking around the perimeter of the topic. From this perspective, you merge with a concept or situation and insights are born out of the experience rather than imposed on it. That's the creative difference.

Unbalanced Expression of Creativity

An unbalanced Fifth Chakra is typified by the person who has awakened to the right for independent thinking, but hasn't any discipline with its expression. If this is you, you will always be opposing other's views, just because "you have the right to." If everybody says yes, you will say no. You are caught up in struggling for your right to be free. Needing to overwhelm opposition in order to verify your view is right, you seek out opportunities to prove this over and over again. You become the nonconformist as a reaction against others, instead of as an open expression of yourself.

When first awakening to this center, it is natural to rebel. against consensus beliefs held by the culture, but problems set in if your ego becomes attached to the alternative views you first settle on. The process freezes. Defensiveness takes over and rigidity in your new beliefs sets in. If you become stuck between having individual thoughts, while simultaneously seeking the approval of others on these views, expect a battlefield. The need to prove that your views are right attracts challenging views from others.

When attachments infiltrate the upper chakras, problems arise. If you become attached to any viewpoint, alternative or conventional, the mind does not experience freedom. An extreme example would be that of the fanatic. Eventually, you realize that fighting for the right to be free doesn't make sense—demanding approval for not needing another's approval? Seeking permission to not ask for permission? This is a bit of a cosmic joke. When you finally get the joke, you let go of constantly needing to be tested in this area, and you can proceed with self-expression. While expressing your right to be independent, you send off a very different energy than if you are looking to prove this right.

Ideally, this rebellion against a consensus mentality leads you to constantly challenge your views as well as the views of others. This allows you to stay open to the process of discovery. This "lens of discovery" allows you to see all truth as relative to what is currently known, and, as a result, you constantly stay open to learning more. Children seem to be particularly open to this creative way of looking at life. Somewhere along the way to adulthood we tend to lose this openness, and balancing the Fifth Chakra is the way to reconnect with this gift.

Another imbalance is inappropriate creativity, as in deception. Stretching the truth is a way of expressing one's self creatively; however, no good comes from it. The intent behind the stretching of the truth determines its positive or negative value. A writer or storyteller embroiders on truth to illustrate a point. A deceitful person is also embellishing truth, but here the motivation is some type of perceived self benefit. The needs of the separate self interfere with the pure creative expression of the Fifth Chakra.

A more common imbalance is not being able to express yourself at all. A feeling of inadequacy can rob your ability to share your views and opinions. It is as if you believe your opinions and attitudes are not valuable, so you hold your tongue instead of taking part in discussions. It is not just *polite listening*, it is truly an *inability to assert your ideas*.

Fearing the consequences of the impact of your ideas on others, you hold back. This leads to feelings of not belonging and feeling like an outsider in most circumstances. You have awakened to independent thinking, but have not accepted the responsibility of giving back to the collective. When you learn to speak up, you will experience a sense of liberation.

Yet another imbalance is an inability to handle the energy itself. Stage fright illustrates this. In this situation your mind is interacting with the collective mind of the audience and experiences the energy as overwhelming. There is very real energy in the group mind of the audience, and it is indeed focused on you. The imbalance occurs when you internalize the experience and try to quell the energy. This can't be done because, like the surfer's wave, the energy is very real.

When speaking before an audience and balanced in the Fifth Chakra, you sense the very same energy, but instead of *internalizing* the energy, you essentially ride the wave and *give the energy back* to the collective. The individual response is taken out of the loop. The first response is the pull of the first three chakras wanting to personalize every experience. In this situation, it is not helpful to be constantly assessing how you feel. Get in the energy and you will be pulled into the group mind and likely find yourself eloquently expressing views you didn't even know you had!

Sustaining a Balanced Creative Level of Consciousness

When you are able to balance the Fifth Chakra, you awaken to original insights by always looking at life with fresh eyes. If you are an artist, your work is original, born out of the moment. If you are in a relationship, your insights keep the relationship constantly alive and growing. If you are in business, you are constantly getting fresh ideas and likely become a successful entrepreneur. Whatever your station in life, you add fresh insights into the situations you are involved with.

This occurs when you are secure in your creative identity to the point of being able to use it when you want, while maintaining the ability to conform to the norm when the situation requires. You are able to see beyond the logical aspects of life, allowing you to draw abstract connections between seemingly unrelated events. Philosophy, politics and religion are likely topics of interest that take you beyond yourself. You are comfortable expressing your ideas with others, even if they can't be backed up with facts; yet, you are not the "know it all" who can't learn from others.

This approach has a refreshing effect on others. You are able to live a creative life and stay balanced in all other areas as well. You probably have chosen some alternative path, as this suits your independent nature. Although your life may be somewhat alternative, others tend to respect your opinion. They can see that your perspective works for you, as your successful life is a testimony.

While most people have an aversion to the intensified energy of the Fifth Chakra, you have learned to be at peace

Your Fifth Chakra

with it. Many types of anxiety and stress stem from resistance to the electrical sensation connected to this level of consciousness.

Exercise 9

To restore balance, focus your attention on your breath. Energy follows breath. Bring your attention to the quality of your breathing and see what you can do to *deepen* and *slow it down*. Notice what happens. Your anxiety subsides and a state of calm alertness possesses you.

Sustaining the fifth level of consciousness requires you to be thoroughly well versed in understanding the nature of universal energy. That is asking a great deal, but you can't swim in the universal waters without awareness of its currents. All the previous chakras must also be balanced so as to not tug your consciousness to lower realms. This allows you to detach from personal reactions to experiences. You begin to work with the energy of a situation and not just its manifestations.

As the Fifth Chakra is in the throat, it has much to do with verbal expression. Speaking your truth is the chief issue here. To sustain this level of consciousness, you must always be able to express your view, even if it is not in accordance with those around you. You become unconcerned whether your views are mainstream or not, or whether they will be accepted or not. Too much adjusting to fit other's views restricts the true expression of the Fifth Chakra.

The highest manifestation of an integrated Fifth Chakra is a free independent mind that knows itself and is not threatened by differences. It is beyond defensiveness, so it is able to entertain any idea with an open and questioning mind. Your consciousness, anchored in creativity, allows looking at life as a field of options. The process leads to the birth of a philosophical view of life.

It is not uncommon that opening to this level of consciousness limits your social world! Many won't be comfortable with your insights, and you won't be comfortable in social situations where trivial thought dominates. As with each of the upper chakras, your desire to spend quality time alone increases as your tolerance for superficial activities decreases.

The Soul's Purpose at the Fifth Chakra

The upper chakras are collective in nature: they connect us to the higher dimension of our species, and beyond. This commingling of individual perspective with the collective mind makes you a fountain of creative insights. The role that evolves as a result of an integrated Fifth Chakra is to serve as an "awakener." You help awaken people from their slumberous thinking. Your insights are "zingers"—they zap people and stimulate them to question their own points of view.

Every culture needs its voices to question it. This questioning keeps a society from becoming stagnant, so those who raise the questioning voices serve the function of helping the culture to evolve. This is your path from the awakened Throat Chakra: to serve as an evolutionary agent in the lives of others.

You serve as a catalyst to others to awaken to their authentic self. People find you challenging, yet exhilarating. Sometimes you are the bearer of unpopular messages, but you are not defensive in the face of other people's reactions to your ideas. You are an idea person and can readily offer alternatives to any situation you consider.

Tips for Awakening Your **FIFTH** *Chakra*

THE FIFTH CHAKRA is useful when you deal with any stage-fright situations. Realize that stage fright and stage presence are exactly the same energy, only how you *respond to the energy* creates the difference. There *is* energy in the situation, so don't try to quiet the energy. Instead, get the separate self out of the way and let the energy move through you.

As a public speaker, I am very familiar with this dynamic. I have always felt a tremendous amount of energy in front of groups. I have been amazed that people would comment on my excitement and enthusiasm, but not on my nervousness. Apparently it didn't show. One time I vowed to quell the nervous energy before a talk. I used yoga breathing and meditation techniques and totally calmed the energy. It was the most boring talk I ever gave! I didn't feel the intense energy, but neither did the audience! The magic was gone. I vowed never to let that happen again and if I don't feel any nervousness or fear before a talk, I pretend I do!

If you have difficulty speaking your truth at the appropriate time, consider the tradition of the "talking stick." In many groups, this tradition is still used. When you have something to say, you ask for the talking stick, and when you have it, everyone else honors this by focusing on what you have to say. Try picturing an invisible talking stick going around the room during a group discussion. When it lands on you, you feel it as the urge to share a view. Honor this invisible talking stick and speak your truth.

Creativity blocks, or "Writer's block," are all too familiar. Use the Fifth Chakra to help you break through these blocks. Imagine working on a creative project of one type or another and you hit the wall of blocked energy. You are likely over-focused on your personal attachment (lower chakra) to the enterprise, which blocks the universal flow. Breathe into your Throat Chakra and then let your creativity fly, unedited. You can edit and polish it later. But to relieve the block, just "let it fly."

The spiritual teacher Ram Dass perhaps most clearly represents an awakened Fifth Chakra. He rebelled against the establishment and challenged conventional thinking. As Richard Alpert, a Harvard professor, he—along with Timothy Leary—began to experiment with the effects of LSD on consciousness. He left his university position and went on a spiritual quest to India, ultimately finding his guru, awakening to his life path, and becoming Ram Dass. At an Omega Institute conference on "Helping Out" in the summer of 1984, he described himself as a "rent-a-mouth for the collective consciousness." By constantly questioning his own beliefs and exploring many of the world's great religions and spiritual paths, he seems to be able to speak what many of us know to be true.

The Desire for Transcendence: Your Sixth Chakra

Color: *Indigo blue*
Crystals: *Fluorite, indigo tourmaline*
Location: *The brow, above the base of the nose*

A HUNGER TO experience the magic and meaning of life, driving you to experience a transcendent reality beyond the everyday view of life heralds the awakening of the Sixth Chakra. Imagination is the vehicle of transcendence. The high road of its use leads to inspiration and bliss, while the low road leads to all forms of escapism. Both roads lead to leaving the everyday reality behind and merging with a larger reality.

This is the world of images, beyond thoughts. The Fifth Chakra translates as mental ideas—the Sixth Chakra is experienced as images and a feeling for a larger life force that you are part of. The desire for transcendence can, of course, be found in a multitude of ways. At the highest level, we can align with the inspirational connection to the Divine through all forms of spiritual practices. We can't always get to the ashram, or an inspirational spot in nature, but we can bring that type of consciousness to even the most mundane experiences—the ability to see the Divine in all things. We can also **draw on** this inspiration through creative activities, such as artistic **expression** as either a patron or performer. It can also be experienced through a magical connection with nature.

A less than high road to transcendence for many people is watching television—and it works. It is not necessarily creative, but it does help one experience an escape from everyday reality. Here, the inherent danger is that people lose their capacity to create this space within themselves. They sacrifice their capacity for transcendence in order to lose themselves in entertainment. Escapism through fantasy is neutral territory—common enough and only troublesome if excessive. The lowest levels of the urge for transcendence are found in drugs and alcohol, deception, deceit, and a life riddled by illusions.

Inspiration to illusion, the Sixth Chakra takes us to a place beyond the limited reality of the senses. It takes spiritual maturity and creative discipline to stay balanced within the Sixth Chakra. The magical mystery world beyond sensory reality has as many madmen as mystics. If your imagination leads you to faith or fear, inspiration or delusion, that is up to you and your discipline.

To discipline your spiritual will, focus on your Sixth Chakra. The normal will of the ego exists in the Third Chakra and, thus, is personal. When you are tired and still have two hours of work left, and you simply *will* yourself to go on, that is Third Chakra power. You also have a spiritual will. Where the personal will directs the activities of the body and mind, the spiritual will focuses on the activities of the spirit. Just as the physical will must be activated to enter

Your Sixth Chakra

into any training of the body, the spiritual will must be activated to enter into training of the spirit.

First, you must recognize the natural tendencies of your imagination when it is not disciplined. What do you tend to fantasize about? What are your natural inclinations with fantasy and imagination? Is your fantasy life dominated by sexual images? Daydreaming? Revenge? Memories? Do you tend to give your fantasy life too much liberty to wander where it may? Or do you stay dominated by the rational mind, thus, not giving your imagination enough opportunity for expression?

To reflect upon your natural tendencies requires the "Witness" point of consciousness. You must collect and synthesize all divergent aspects of yourself and unite them into a single point of awareness. The goal is to develop a point of reflection in your life that can witness even your own involvement with life, as it is happening. To be "in the world, but not of the world" is the object.

The vantage point of the Witness is the first step of developing spiritual will. Observe any fluctuations in your energy field while you are engaging your imagination. Are you experiencing a subtle *depletion,* or *enhancement,* of your energy? The Witness is able to discern, by observing your own energy field, if the imagination is moving in healthy or unhealthy directions.

The active expression of the spiritual will comes next when you must extract your attention from that which is depleting your energy, and direct it to that which *enhances* your energy. What inspires you? Develop the discipline to aim your attention in that direction. Awakening into energy consciousness requires you to trust that following that which enhances your energy is your correct path.

Directed imagery, or creative visualization, is the method for swimming in the waters beyond the self. Be cautious of the questioning mind. "This can't be right." "It is only my imagination," etc. This doubting mind is like a guardian at the gate, pulling one back to earthbound consciousness. You have to learn to quiet this voice and put it to rest. This is done through the spiritual will by pulling your attention away from the questioning mind, and leading it to the calm, quiet center from which inspiration is born.

As you continue to work with this energy, your intuition sharpens. Let's say your *trust* in your intuition sharpens. Intuition is always operating—the question is whether you are listening to it or not. Intuition is experienced as a type of knowing beyond strategic thinking. You first start becoming aware of your intuition as an "Advance Warning System"—it gives you a clue when danger is present. You can sense when something is not quite right, even if everything seems quite fine to your normal senses. If you ignore the alarm and continue on your set course, even though your intuition warns you not to, you soon learn to listen! When a problem arises, you eventually remember the voice that knew all along that something was amiss.

This warning type of intuition develops along the lines of reaction to potential danger. Useful, but limited. A pro-active path can also be developed. This essentially results from aiming your intuition at an idea or concept and trusting the creative genius of the collective mind to help you see it in a new way. Being intuitively pro-active engages the experience rather than waiting for its alarm function. Intuition applied at work, in relationships and in creativity, offers a tremendous advantage. The positive expression of your intuition express itself in the moment as a sense of a spiritual signature in the situation before you, and you *know* it has special significance.

The knowing of the Sixth Chakra gift is experienced as sensing if your current path is aligned with your true path or not. When you are aligned, you can feel the elastic pull of your true path's subtle magnetic currents. You become skilled at seeing and interpreting the omens you receive as messages from the larger life force. When a choice is presented, you can simply feel if the elastic connection is there or not. This tells you whether the choice is part of your true path.

The imagination, without the spiritual will attending to it, creates random experiences of both fear and faith. Some people get stuck in these fears, which serve as the guardians to the gate, repelling one from further progress. The emotion of fear is dominant in human consciousness, so there is plenty around to experience. You have to know how to dispel fears through using the spiritual will to steer away from this energy, and toward the light of faith.

This is easy to describe, but can be difficult to master. We have very little cultural training for engaging the spiritual will. Our culture, in fact, seems to promote fear. Many of the world's religions actively promote the idea that this life is a fall from Divine grace, the afterlife will be much better, and without the protection of religion, one could end up in hell. These teachings obviously play on the fear factor.

Even if you do not personally believe in these religious doctrines, you should still take them into account when dealing with collective levels of reality. All of the upper chakras deal with the collective consciousness, so understanding the impact of these collective beliefs is similar to understanding the currents of a particular waterway before heading off in a boat. By understanding the nature of the collective beliefs, you can be prepared for the currents you will have to navigate through at this level of consciousness. You must break through the dense energy of fear to get to the higher vibration of faith.

Another chief characteristic of this level of consciousness is becoming aware of a larger reality that one can draw energy from. The Tao, or "Way" of Eastern mysticism, pictured as a river of life that we are all a part of, becomes a tangible reality. (The Tao will be explained further in the following section.) Faith in a larger reality changes from a belief system, as held in the lower chakras, to an "experience" at this level. You are able to perceive the workings of the Divine and to align with it.

The Transcendent Perspective

When one rises to the Sixth Chakra, or Third-Eye level of consciousness, the ability to transcend polarity is born. Before you awaken to this center, polarity consciousness is the norm. Something is either right or wrong, good or bad. If there are differences of opinions, one has to be right, the other wrong. From the sixth center of consciousness, you rise above polarity and see life through a larger lens that encompasses all views. This is the "unitive state of consciousness," where all appears as the many manifestations of the One Great Spirit. The experience of bliss accompanies this perspective. Not much ruffles or surprises you, since your view of life transcends and includes all polarities.

Looking at life through the Sixth Chakra allows you to sense a greater reality occurring beyond your individual will. You feel the currents of the larger life force. Most spiritual traditions encourage you to develop the perspective of the Sixth Chakra. Christian mystics refer to this as the "Witness;" J. Krishnamurti referred to this as the "Detached Observer;" the Buddhists name this the point of "mindfulness." You develop the point of consciousness that can observe yourself, even while in action—you are involved, and aware of the involvement, simultaneously.

This perspective on life is also well described as the way of the Tao (The *Tao Te Ching* by Lao Tzu), simply described as the flow of the larger life force that we are part of. As you begin to sense this interaction between your individual life force and the universal life force, your faith becomes empowered. The Tao is invisible, but absolutely discernible if you are attuned to it. As you get better at aligning with it, your life seems to move forward effortlessly, as if you were being pulled along by some unseen current.

When you follow the Tao, you understand the path of effortless action. The saying, "Without doing anything, leave nothing undone," expresses this well. To our personal mind, this saying makes no sense whatsoever. The Sixth Chakra perspective allows you to enter into the activity being done, instead of doing it. You are able to interact with the task being done through you, rather than imposing your personal will on the situation. This subtle distinction is what the path of "effortless action" is all about.

The Sixth Chakra perspective takes you to the astral plane, and you are advised to know your way around this level of collective consciousness if you are to spend time there. If this were a golden time in human history, the involvement with the astral plane would be glorious. But we live in troubled times, and as a result, the astral plane is also troubled, with as much fear, perversion, guilt, and shame as inspired energy. One must be discriminating. This requires the development of the spiritual will and learning how to influence the direction of your imagination.

This is no small trick to attempt by yourself. Spiritual and religious communities provide support and structure for staying vigilant within the realms you allow yourself to imagine. Many individuals are able to maintain a personal practice, outside of religion, of staying aligned with their spiritual will. Some form of meditation or prayer, as a central theme within the practice, is likely. The practice of worship fosters inspiration from a Sixth Chakra perspective. Reading inspired literature and listening to visionary speakers also works.

For those who have found the creative dimension of the Sixth Chakra, becoming absorbed in the creative process becomes the form of worship and also works to keep one aligned with inspiration. For nature lovers, this absorption and surrender happens with nature and becomes their form of worship.

Unbalanced Expression of Transcendence

Imbalances in this chakra are typically caused by the imagination disassociating from mundane reality. Getting lost in the "non-reality" realms of the astral plane where fear, escapism, illusions, and all other "imagination-run-wild" scenarios are the consequences of this imbalance. The imagination is clearly operating, but in a disempowering way.

The most common unbalanced use of the Sixth Chakra is allowing yourself to be engulfed by fear. It takes skill to navigate beyond the fear realms, because they are dominant everywhere around us. Fear is meant to be a "standby" alarm system, not a state of consciousness. When you feel fear at the sound of a car at the street corner, and you instinctively pull back, it is serving you. But when fear is not on standby, instead it is constantly sounding, this is to be *engulfed by fear*. Then fear has its say in all the choices you make.

Until you have developed the Witness, the capacity to discern the quality of your imaginary experience is not present. To practice the use of your spiritual will, you must first develop the capacity to discern the impact of your imaginative wanderings on your energy field. If you can't tell the difference in the moment, you would not know how to direct your will. The first key then, in getting beyond imbalances such as fear, is being able to discern whether or not you are in a state of balance.

You are in troubled waters when you get so immersed in the fear, you can't tell you are off-center. It all looks real to you. If, at least, you know you are off-balance, then you can track your attention to the place within you that knows. Ah, you are no longer engulfed in fear! If you have developed the Witness, this comes naturally. You can read your own energy field to know if you are in a state of inspiration or illusion, fear or faith, creativity or escapism.

The key is to assess the quality of your energy in the moment. Do you feel inspired and filled with subtle energy? Or do you feel drained by fear? Do you feel a contraction and tightening in your energy field, or expansive and opening? The measure of balance is found within you. Read your own energy.

Some people encounter specific entities in the imaginary realms that embody their own fears. These are akin to the nightmares of youth. These entities have a real presence, so it is not adequate to simply dismiss them as figments of your imagination. If you run across one of the entities in your wanderings, it is best to actually interact with the entity and dismiss it directly. Let it know that you won't be bullied. They always back down in the face of strength, so this is where the spiritual will comes in again. Instincts want to propel you away from the feared object, but the spiritual will must override these impulses and, guided by faith, give you the strength to face the fear, dismiss it, and move on to higher realms.

The imbalance of the Sixth Chakra creates distorted vision. A chief culprit here is over reliance on drugs and alcohol. This creates a pseudo-Third-Eye experience of an altered view of reality, but it is distorted. It is also quite possible to experience distorted vision without any stimulants at all. This would most typically occur if you have not integrated the lessons of the previous chakras. Like the bewilderment of Alice as she was falling through the looking glass, the unbalanced sixth center is one of confused vision instead of inspiration.

The results of this distortion could run the gamut from a belief that the self is special and above all others, to an attachment to your special cross to bear that no one else is aware of. In both cases, the pull of the personal is still interfering with the pure experience of recognizing the Divinity in all of life.

What is not part of the whole? Any exclusivity cannot lead to the whole, thus attachments to any religion or doctrine as the only truth, of course *limits,* rather than *expands* perspective. Even personal prejudices and biases must be seen, identified, and gone beyond to have a clear transcendent perspective. Over-awareness of where you and others are in relation to spiritual development can also be a sign of imbalance, i.e., "I do yoga, and she doesn't—I must be more spiritually evolved than she." Spiritual development isn't a race.

Guilt is another manifestation of an unbalanced Sixth Chakra. This usually stems from a philosophical/religious belief held in the Fifth Chakra that still leads to dualistic thinking. There is a separation between self and the Divine

Your Sixth Chakra

resulting in a belief that you are unworthy. Here, again, the separate, personal sense of self butts in where it doesn't belong and brings the attention back to the self; the self in its unworthiness, but self just the same.

The root of all suffering is separation from the Divine. The suffering is meant to be a warning that you are moving in an unhealthy direction with this energy. Listen to the warning by vowing to align with the cure for all suffering—a connection to the Divine. Find it in your own way, but find it.

Being "spaced out" is another obvious distortion from this lens. You are merging with the infinite, but at inappropriate times and in inappropriate ways. In this condition, you are able to develop the Witness within to watch your interaction with life, but being unbalanced, you can't interact with normal reality in a conscientious way. The prime example are those who only use drugs to open this center. While they are under the influence of a drug, they are able to step back and witness life, but other people find them hard to reach and usually feel unsatisfied interacting with them.

It doesn't just take drugs to get one distorted, however. Obsessive sexual fantasizing certainly skews one's perception, and this is an example of how an imbalance in a lower chakra interferes with the upper chakras. Although the fantasizing is clearly of the Sixth, the sexual content, from an unbalanced Second Chakra, is fueling the activity. Another example of an unbalanced Sixth Chakra is the person who can't separate imagination from reality, as is the case with the person who imagines qualities in others they can't possibly live up to, or falls in love with qualities in the other that are not even there!

Excessive sensitivity to all worldly stimulation can happen if you haven't balanced the physical chakras on the way up to opening your Third Eye. This vibrational sensitivity can manifest as all types of environmental illnesses and sensitivities: From the electro-magnetic energy fields of electricity transformers, to the pesticides and chemicals of food, to the products used in building supplies, to traffic fumes, to the harshness of everyday life in our modern world. I do not want to imply that everyone with environmental illnesses is unbalanced in the lower chakras. This is clearly not the case, but it is certainly something to investigate. Those suffering from a reaction to the environment may very well be the canaries in the coalmine who alarm us all to how toxic our environment is becoming. Many with these sensitivities are being lead to lifestyles with a purified vibrational field.

Sustaining a Balanced Transcendent Level of Consciousness

From this state of consciousness you experience the bliss of seeing the Divine perfection in all things. It is as if you are a cell of consciousness in the greater consciousness of Mother Earth. You are in touch with the Tao and, thus, can sense its currents and readily align with them. Being in harmony with this inspired point of view leads to a life of great ease and enjoyment. You might seem psychic to others, but to yourself, you are just watching the currents of this more comprehensive life force and can ride its many changes. This gives you prophetic insight—by seeing into the subtle levels of energy—you sense the movement in the energy before it becomes manifest.

Through slow, steady and patient work, you have developed a rapport with the Witness within, allowing you to objectively watch while you are interacting with others. The ability to remain detached, while still being involved, gives you wisdom and insights into the meaning of life.

Being balanced in the Sixth Chakra allows you to sense a larger flow of reality and, as you align with it, your intuition blossoms. You readily adapt to situations that are beyond your personal control. Just knowing how much of life exists beyond your control is evidence of a life force beyond the individual, and you trust that aligning with this universal life force is in your best interest.

Your faith is strengthened as you see the fruits of following the path beyond self, for everything that the self previously wanted, now seems to be available. Without effort, your needs are being met, freeing you to attend to the awareness of the greater life force around you. Faith is not based on belief, it is anchored in experience. You seem to have an uncanny knack for being in the right place at the right time without necessarily planning it. By listening to the still, quiet voice within, your intuition allows you to see the signs and omens that reveal your path.

You can have Sixth Chakra experiences without a spiritual practice, but you cannot sustain this level of consciousness without a disciplined spiritual will. Without discipline, the awakened Third Eye is as delusional as it is inspirational, leading to random transcendent experiences, some based in fear and some based in faith. You are like a ship without a rudder in this sea of the collective imagination. As you develop the discernment of knowing if your wanderings are enhancing or depleting your energy, you begin to direct your attention to the inspirational. This is the spiritual will.

A practice of one type or another is required to direct the attention to this transcendent and inspired view of life.

Often, this becomes absorbing and many who experience this develop lifestyles that allow for more constant experience of the Divine. Ashram life, a yoga lifestyle, a dedicated religious or spiritual practice, a deep spiritual connection with nature, an artistic lifestyle with much opportunity to let creativity flow through you, are examples of Sixth Chakra lifestyles.

By learning to stay balanced at this level of consciousness, you become a visionary. Seeing beyond the mind, beyond words, you see in pictures, images, intuitions. You are guided by a higher voice and inspire others to listen to this voice within themselves. You have no doctrine to promote, nor any particular teaching to offer—your vision is beyond such distinctions. Your ability to live a life of great peace is your teaching.

Rising above polarity translates as an ability to rise above conflict. Conflict results because of a rigid adherence to conflicting views. By being able to see a larger reality that encompasses the polarities, you are able to rise above the conflicts and live a life of peace. Even in the middle of all the chaos and violence of our modern world, the balanced opening of the Third Eye allows you to adhere to another reality, which is not attached to the conflict levels.

A sense of the deeper meaning behind all manifest reality reveals itself to you with balance here. You align your desires with that which is unfolding and your life seems blessed. Magic is not uncommon in your life. There seems to be a pixie dust quality to all that you do, at least, from the perspective of others. To you, however, you are simply aligning with a life current that is larger than the personal.

This flow of energy from the larger reality into one's individual reality is experienced as inspiration, thus the ability to be inspired and to inspire others are side benefits of this alignment. Curiously, it is not the "I" that is inspiring others. To draw on inspiration, you need to transcend the separate "I" level of consciousness. Then, when the "I" intercedes and you become insecure and shrink away from the role of helping others, you can laugh at that "I" voice. Reassure it that it is not the "I" that is going to do the work anyway! It is aligning with the inspirational level of consciousness, in and of itself, that inspires others.

The Soul's Purpose at the Sixth Chakra

You have developed a wisdom that comes from a perspective that transcends polarity and can help others see the deeper meaning of the situations in their lives—and, likely, they seek you out for this. Your range of perspective has expanded to the degree that you see many more variables impinging on any moment than most people. You are called to help others awaken to an expanded perspective of their lives and possibilities. This stimulates a sense of vision in others—the vision that there is more to life than simply surviving. You offer others a perspective that frees them from limited views on reality. Others may think of you as psychic or insightful, and your intuition is uncanny compared to this dulled faculty in the general public.

You are always able to help others find a higher path beyond their current dilemma. Your perspective can be like a nectar that satisfies a thirst for the Divine in others. You become a fountain of spiritual wisdom and are able to see the laws of creation manifesting before your eyes. Seeing everything as it is, as the perfect consequence of that which has gone on before, you also see the possibilities that this presents. As a visionary, you focus less on issues at hand and more on possibilities.

*Tips for Awakening Your **SIXTH** Chakra*

WHEN YOU FEEL lost and adrift without direction or purpose, focus on your Sixth Chakra and start looking for meaning in your life. Teachers abound; are you listening? Look for omens, ask for signs, seek direction and interaction with your higher self. Use the oracles like the I–Ching, tarot cards, medicine cards, or runes, and ask for direction. If you approach these tools in a sacred manner, they will provide a vehicle for your higher self to express itself to you.

Court this chakra by listening to inspirational speakers (in person or on tape), and reading the material that fills you with faith and vision. Simply said, to add more meaning to your life, look for more meaning in your life. Go to the sources.

In conflict situations, within yourself or with others, have faith in a transcendent view and find the vantage point that sees a larger reality that both polarities are part of. Know in your heart that a way beyond polarity exists and then allow yourself, even force yourself, to find that perspective. Solutions always exist, the high road is always available—remembering there is a way beyond conflict is the fist step. Know that if you attend to this vantage point, the high road will reveal itself.

When you are depressed and lacking spirit, learn how to invite spirit in. Understand Divine discontent for what it is. Yogananda, one of the great spiritual teachers, wrote a great deal about Divine discontent. He said that much of our suffering and grief is caused by a separation from God. The hunger is for divine connection, but we often think that something else is missing in our lives. This is Divine discontent—misplaced search for a spiritual connection has us looking in our worldly life for something it can't provide. The next time you are depressed, consider this principle of Divine discontent and see if a search for your spiritual source doesn't resolve the issue.

Exercise 10

A Meditation: Sit or lie down with your spine straight. Breathe deep and slow to calm yourself. Notice the subtle rising and falling of your energy on each breath to focus your attention. Once you are centered, imagine the ocean in all of its vastness. Immerse yourself in the feeling of being part of this great vastness. You are not in it and separate from it, you are it—become it. Now, experience an individual wave rising up out of the ocean. See this as your individual life—separate and distinct, yet part of it all. See the rising and falling of the waves as your incarnations. Rising up out of the ocean, your individual life is born, only to fall back into the oneness. And yet another wave rises and another of your incarnations emerges to express itself and falls again to merge with the all. How many times has the wave of an individual life risen for you? How many times in the future will it rise again? Feel the vastness of the possibilities.

As you feel the cresting and falling of each wave, feel the embrace of the ocean as it welcomes you back home. Picture this as merging with the Divine. Feel how compassionate the Divine is, always welcoming you back into itself. See what an illusion any sense of separateness is. The wave is still part of the ocean, the ocean is within the wave. Any feelings of separateness are an illusion—*feel* your connection to the eternal vastness.

The Surrender to Spirituality: Your Seventh Chakra

Color: *Violet or white*
Crystals: *Clear quartz*
Location: *The crown of the head*

BY DEFINITION, THE Crown Chakra represents pure, undifferentiated cosmic energy. The desire to experience the Divine, however you define this, is the dominant drive of the Seventh Chakra. If there is a need, it is to absolutely surrender to Divine guidance. At this level, we are not satisfied knowing about the spiritual life, we want to merge with the Divine and have all of our actions guided by this union.

This chakra, which started the process of involution, receiving the energy, is the same chakra that completes the process of evolution. The energy that has been borrowed from the universe to animate your life, is now given back to unite the personal experiences with the collective. This is your offering to the universe—an energetic sum total of all that you are.

When you have awakened to this level, all of life is seen as a spiritual experience. You see the Divine smiling back at you from all of reality. Your life is marked by a quality of reverence in that you realize the sacred dimension of all experiences.

Although it is Divine grace that ultimately bestows this experience on us, we can prepare ourselves in readiness by leading a life with sacred awareness. This courts the experience of enlightenment and illumination. Enlightenment is not permanent. It is most likely a fleeting glimpse of this highest level of reality, there for a moment and then gone. It comes when it comes, but we can increase the likelihood of its occurrence with meditation, prayer and deep contemplation.

The Spiritual Perspective

This is total hook up. Rare experiences for most of us and only a precious few individuals throughout history have been able to sustain conscious awareness from this perspective. These are the angelic beings who have totally surrendered individual consciousness to the Divine. For most of us, it is the "peak," or "oceanic," experience of sudden total awareness. This is looking at life from the perspective of the Divine looking through your eyes.

This is the fruit of living a sacred life. Merging with the infinite allows you to see into the souls of others. How you respond to this information will determine how long you are able to sustain this level of perspective. If this seeing triggers a fear response, you will be immediately repelled back into the lower chakras where you feel safer. To remain centered at this level is no small task. Knowing carries a price. You awaken to full memory; you *know*. There is a required level of surrender to sustain the Seventh Chakra perspective.

Each of us has a purpose; the Divine intent that brought us into incarnation. There is a sense of purpose with each of the upper chakras, but the Seventh Chakra awakens us to the all-encompassing purpose of the soul for this life. When you awaken into full Seventh Chakra perspective, there is no denying your purpose and this knowledge carries a responsibility. Accept or deny it? There is choice here. If you deny your awareness of your purpose, again you are repelled back to the lower chakras. If you accept, you tap into a source of energy that is inexhaustible. All of the energy and circumstances that you need to fulfill your soul's purpose are provided by the Divine.

When living a Seventh Chakra perspective, you may prefer to be alone with nature and your spiritual contemplations, but others definitely want to be with you. Giving to others from this perspective, fortunately, comes naturally, being that you are tapped into the universal life force of inexhaustible energy. To sustain this perspective you must be able to stay aligned with the Divine at all times. When you break the connection and others continue to draw from you, you end up relying on your personal energy, not the Divine source. Eventually, with such a depletion, your personal energy wanes and you are drawn into the lower chakras.

Unbalanced Spiritual Expression

This chakra is a dangerous place to be unbalanced. It can lead to a life anchored in a separate reality, very real to you, but not integrated with the world around you. This causes a disassociation with mundane reality and an inability to interact with the everyday world in an effective way.

Imbalance here can lead to confrontations with the guardians to the final gate, or the embodiments of your fears that manifest as entities that seem to haunt you. Although, from the worldly perspective, these seem to be phantom ghosts of little consequence, for the person confronting these energies, they are very real. Aligning with the teachings from any of the world's sacred texts is a perfect antidote for those wandering into the fear zones of the Seventh Chakra. The Bible, the Koran, The I–Ching, the Tao Te Ching, the Upanishads, the Bhagavad Gita and many others, are tools for bringing the self into alignment at this highest level.

I suspect that many who are in asylums are open at this universal level, but with no connection to the lower chakras and the personal self. They are living in a separate reality without the grounding of the lower chakras.

Another imbalance here is what I call the "Shopping List" mentality. New Age teachings speak of creating a mock-up of how you want your life to be. If you want a relationship or a new job, you are advised to write down a list of your specific requests and meditate on this as if it were true. This undoubtedly works, as those who have experienced it will testify. Still, it is the ego that is making the list and when the ego gets involved in upper chakras, balance cannot be achieved. It is the ego saying that it knows more about its needs than God does. Instead of absolutely surrendering to the flow of your life, you are busy attempting to direct it. This denies much of the magic that can happen when you totally surrender to the Divine plan.

The simple mantra, "Let go and let God (Goddess)" can be the perfect antidote for those having difficulty letting go of control in their lives. It is an interesting process. At the first level of awakening to higher levels of consciousness, you must regain control of your life by taking responsibility for all of your experiences. This is necessary to break free from the cultural conditioning you have been exposed to. At the first level, this taking charge of life is a necessary step.

However, if one is to experience the highest levels of awareness, control must be released to the Divine. First regain your authentic self by taking control, but ultimately, surrender to the highest force you believe in to anchor yourself in the Divine.

Sustaining a Balanced Spiritual Level of Consciousness

The Seventh Chakra consciousness level is best described as sacred. Surrender to the Highest is total and all of life is aligned with Divine Will. To achieve this level of consciousness requires absolute surrender to this higher power. You have absolutely no question as to your path; you are living it, constantly. You are in this world, but not of this world, because your consciousness is anchored with Divine awareness.

In the Buddhist tradition, the path of the Bodhisattva describes this level of awareness. The Bodhisattva is one who has achieved personal enlightenment but, instead of leaving this world to experience eternal bliss, vows to stay until suffering ends. Awakening to the Seventh Chakra is awakening to the path of the Bodhisattva.

Accompanying this level of consciousness is the awareness of eternity. In this state you become aware that you will have to answer for all your actions for eternity. That is how much time we have to get it right. When you realize that the law of cause and effect stays in effect for eternity, you start putting energy toward getting it right. There is no tricking the place of Divine awareness within you; some part of you knows if you are in alignment with your highest self or not. Finally giving up all the ways of hiding from your Divine Awareness, you surrender to a life animated by the highest intentions, and stay constantly vigilant to maintain this perspective.

Before you learn to maintain this level of awareness through your own efforts, it exists as Grace. The Seventh Chakra is just beyond our reach. It can be experienced, but not by personal volition, at least not in the normal sense of willful endeavors. It is most often experienced as Divine intervention without personal prompting. These peak experiences are quite rare. Brief flashes of Divine awareness, as if the soul of the cosmos opens up and breathes into you. These brief and sporadic "inbreaths" from the Divine often change one's life.

After you have felt the charge of this total hookup, everything else pales in significance. Your hunger for this experience can begin to supplant all other drives, and your quest for the Divine realization begins in earnest. You do not just want to know *about* God, you want to know God! This single-pointed attention eventually bears fruit, and you begin to spend more and more of your time anchored in Divine Awareness.

What cannot be known until this happens is that it is not a path of sacrifice as popularly thought. To sustain this level of consciousness requires all of the previous chakras to be integrated and balanced, which rules out sacrifice. Actually, if sacrifice is involved, the energies of the chakra being denied ultimately pull your attention to the missing piece of the puzzle, and your attention is drawn to the very source you are attempting to renounce.

Surrender should not be confused with sacrifice. Sacrifice implies letting go of something that you value, but what is actually required is to trust that as you surrender your life to the Divine, all you value will come into alignment as well.

We are meant to be fully animated beings. Surrendering to the highest voice that you believe in leads to the ultimate

Seventh Chakra state of consciousness. It is a way of living life that is absolutely in everyone's best interest, including the self. There is a way of living life that doesn't promote endless suffering. There is a way of living life that causes harm to no one, and yet is not about sacrifice, which actually causes harm to the separate self. Sacrifice implies that everyone else's needs are more important than your own. Surrendering allows you to discover a path that is in everyone's best interest, including your own.

This deserves some exploration. The Seventh Chakra level of consciousness is the full awareness that All Is One: Everything comes from the same Divine emanation. When you enter into sacrifice, it is a form of spiritual suicide. This denial of the self is a denial of part of the Divine's creation, which is against the basic principle of the Seventh level. You cannot sustain this level of consciousness with sacrifice of the self. To align with this center means to allow for the total integration and enhancement of all the chakras; the ego, the soul and the spirit are all fully animated and alive.

Imbalances here are often caused by aligning with false gurus and inappropriate teachings. The true Seventh Chakra level of consciousness is a direct connection with the Divine—no intermediaries. It is possible that in your eagerness to live in Divine Awareness, you accept teachers, manifestoes, dogmas and other intermediaries as if they were God. If the path you are surrendering to fills you with inspiration and brings you closer to your higher self and the Divine, trust it. If your path does not fill you with inspiration and faith, or get you closer to your higher self or the Divine, be suspicious. Be patient and wait for the real thing. It is worth the wait—but don't wait in emptiness, wait in full anticipation of this eventual Divine connection and it will happen.

To live in full Seventh Chakra consciousness is the ultimate act of faith. Faith in knowing what lies beyond the fear is paramount. The first time through the limited realm of individual consciousness into the limitless expanse of spiritual reality, one has to go on blind faith, simply believing that there is reality beyond the fear. These are the Magellans of consciousness: those having faith they won't fall off the end of the world by going beyond the known.

Beyond fear is freedom. Without the yoke of fear, one is free to experience the awareness of the universal life energy flowing through all of creation, for all time. This brings liberation and true freedom—freedom from limiting and restricting views of reality.

Imagine what this does to your sense of time! Impatience drops. When you are aware of eternity, what does a few minutes here or there matter? The linear sense of time that is perceived from the lower chakras dissolves into an awareness of circular time. You realize that you have all of the time in the world for all that needs to be done. Time becomes an ally and a friend rather than a competitor. You learn to cherish the moment. Patience blossoms.

Freedom allows you to experience the life force coursing through the veins of all existence, to explore dimensions of life outside the body, and to know this universal realm exists. This knowing changes one's life. It is no longer simply faith in a reality beyond fear, it has become a direct experience. Knowing the truth of this experience and knowing that it is accessible changes your relationship with all life.

Study the lives of the holy ones: Jesus, Buddha, Lao Tzu, Mother Teresa, Gandhi, Yogananda, Thich Nhat Hanh, Muktananda, to name a few. What is the common thread? Absolute connection to the Divine—constantly. The limited list of those who have sustained balance at this level is a testimony of the enormity of the task. To move the center of one's consciousness to the Divine consciousness, while simultaneously staying centered in personal consciousness, is a difficult task.

Your surrender to the Divine will must to be complete—you can't barter with God. Ask yourself: are you prepared to do what it takes to align totally with Divine will? Or do you tend to harbor secret conditions involving surrender. "I will completely surrender to the Divine's will as long as I get to stay with my husband, my family stays intact, I get to keep good health, have a reasonable income and a nice place to live . . ." I'm exaggerating slightly, but the point is, there is no bargaining. You either surrender completely or you don't.

Here is the paradox of all paradoxes. When the ego finally gives up its control and surrenders to the Divine's will, you most often get everything the ego would have wanted and more! You can't know this ahead of time; you have to go with the honest faith that the Divine knows best. Most people report that when they finally do surrender, they effortlessly receive everything their ego was afraid of losing before the surrender. Of course, they may also get more than their ego could have even known existed. Don't limit the Divine by assuming you know more about what is in your ultimate best interest.

This gets compounded when other people are involved, particularly if you are married or have children. Your responsibility is on the line. You may feel that you must maintain control for the sake of everyone you love. This presents a real test of faith. Is your faith strong enough for you believe that no one you love could ever be hurt by your following your highest path? It takes profound strength of faith when others are involved.

I have my own story of surrendering. Before I became a full-time astrologer, my wife and I owned and operated a restaurant. I enjoyed the work, but it was not my passion. Astrology and the spiritual path were my passions. However, I didn't believe I could support my four sons on an astrologer's pay. The restaurant provided an adequate salary, plus the security of the huge refrigerator if times got bad. I did my astrology on the side whenever I had the chance, but restaurants tend to consume time, so astrology was not the dominant activity of my life.

I heard the call from within that it was time to let go of the restaurant and dedicate all my energies to being an astrologer. I resisted the voice with the argument that my family needed security. The voice continued and I continued to resist with noble indignation, because I had to provide for my family after all!

Then, a particularly strong and pivotal week arrived. As fate would have it, I saw three different clients with similar issues that week. Each was an artist of one type or another, but they had other jobs to support themselves. Typically I consider myself a gentle counselor, so I was quite surprised when I found myself yelling at the third client: "You can't call yourself an artist, you are really a clerk! That is what you are dedicating most of your time to, and being a clerk is what you are getting better at doing because you are putting your energy into being a clerk, not your art."

After she left, I sat stunned by my reaction; I suspected I had also yelled at myself. The message was for me. I couldn't call myself an astrologer if I put most of my time into the restaurant. I was getting better at the restaurant business, not astrology. My wife and I decided to sell our share of the business to our partner to allow me to dedicate full time to astrology. We had enough savings from the sale to cushion us for a while, so I gave myself a year to get back to the accustomed income. I figured that if astrology didn't pan out as a viable career after one year, I could always start another restaurant.

We moved to a small town on the Olympic Peninsula where we didn't know anybody, but we liked the feel of the country. I was not at all prepared for what happened. I gave myself a year to get back to the same level of income as before, but it only took one month! In the first year, my income actually doubled! I couldn't figure it out for the life of me. It seemed like the ultimate paradox: The whole time I was attached to money for security, instead of aligning with my faith, I was essentially holding back my income by half!

Since then, this lesson has been shown to me over and over. These experiences have revealed to me the meaning of the saying: "Seek ye first the kingdom of Heaven inside yourself, and then all things will be added upon you."

The Soul's Purpose at the Seventh Chakra

Until we are awakened at the Seventh Chakra, we use many methods to get to the spiritual. Once we align with the Divine, *all of life* is a spiritual path. You need the methods until you get there, but once aligned with the Divine, you are already there, and the need for practice to get there diminishes. Your purpose is to demonstrate the way back into life.

Spiritual paths of all sorts teach the path of letting go of material attachments in favor of Divine awareness. It is a necessary step to reject attachments—the path of renunciation. But once awakened, you now bring this awareness into all areas of life—family, career, everything. It's like the saying, "Before enlightenment, chop wood, carry water. After enlightenment, chop wood, carry water." Your purpose is a testimony that all of life is spiritual practice.

Tips for Awakening Your **SEVENTH** *Chakra*

WHEN LIFE IS desperate, try desperate measures. Absolute surrender. Go ahead and totally give up, but give up with faith. At least believe in the possibility, that if you absolutely give up personal volition, you make way for a higher power to come through you. Your old way is obviously not working, so why not give it a try? The moment of despair can become the eye of the needle that you pass through to experience this highest level of connection.

But then, why wait for despair? It does work as a driving force to get us to search for the Divine, but why not do this *before* despair sets in? This is the attitude of the visionary. Why not engage this level of consciousness *out of choice*, instead of being driven to it? Then things change from desperate need, to gracious opportunity!

Section III
Essays

The Dance of Ego, Soul, and Spirit

THE DANCE OF ego, soul, and spirit takes place within the chakras. It can be seen that the ego, the separate identity of the self, is animated by the energy of the first three chakras. The Soul is the Heart Chakra, with allegiance to both ego and spiritual realms. Spirit infuses the upper chakras. The ideal is that each chakra integrates its gifts and perspectives with all the others. Growing in consciousness is knowing more of the territory of your being, ultimately expanding to encompass all of the chakras simultaneously. Ultimate awareness. Not easy to obtain, however, because of attachments. Attachments limit, hold and freeze consciousness to certain points of view, perspectives and opinions. Attachments are natural; they spontaneously arise, but it must be seen that they will contaminate the experience of oneness by putting the self where it doesn't belong.

We needn't kill the ego. That's not the point—it has its healthy role in the big picture, just as soul and spirit do. The ideal is to expand your view beyond the ego's range, which is narrow by definition. It is an accumulation of opinions, thoughts, attitudes, values and emotions of the self. The ego, by definition, is prejudiced by what supports its views and discriminates against all else. When it wanders into the upper chakras, problems are always going to arise, because the ego simply hasn't the capacity to consider a universal view. It is designed for personal view. The ego and its accompanying attachments are most often the source of problems attending the upper chakras.

It doesn't seem to do much good to slay or repress the ego. This just leads to self-esteem problems, which limit your ability to enjoy life. It is obviously best to have a healthy ego and, just as important, to know its limits. Creating a strong, well-balanced self-identity by developing the first three chakras creates a strong personality and presence. A healthy ego is good, in and as far as it goes, but its limits of effectiveness are exclusively within the realms of the first three chakras. Personal style, taste, values and emotions all come from these realms. Earthly activities give the ego plenty to lord over, but it shouldn't go beyond its natural domain. When it does, it always tries to make personal that which is not.

To move beyond the limited view of the first three chakras does not require going against the perspectives they bring, simply beyond them. Moving beyond means to delve into the conscious awareness of the soul. The soul is always there, of course, but our conscious awareness of it may not be. The center of consciousness has to shift in order to allow the awakening of the heart, the seat of the soul. You have to be able to take that leap of faith of believing that it is safe to lower your defenses. That one leap is a mighty leap, however, because it allows you to bring the heart into your life experiences. Life without heart is a tough experience. Awakening to the heart softens life and allows joy—the song of the soul—to be present.

Awakening to the soul's experience of life through the Fourth Chakra is not a linear shift up some scale. It is more

The Dance of Ego, Soul, and Spirit

like changing one's focus to allow a larger concentric circle to be experienced beyond a previously limited view. The ideal is to expand your perspective to a larger reality, while still maintaining clarity of perspective through the first three chakras.

To continue to expand takes you to the level of spirit and collective awareness. You begin to understand that individual consciousness is born out of the larger collective consciousness of Mother Earth. As a cell within Gaia, you sense an intimate connection with all existence. Greater acceptance of your role in the scheme of things always blossoms from here, plus it brings the gift of freedom; freedom to not react in defensive, reactionary ways. Freedom to explore consciousness by rising above polarized views.

The first of the upper chakras brings us to the higher perspective of the mind. The analogy of your mind representing a personal computer and the Fifth Chakra representing the mainframe, from which all personal computers draw their information, is a worthy image. In this analogy, you have access to the big computer in the sky from which all thoughts are derived. It can be seen that each individual, through the workings of the lower three chakras, creates his or her personal experience of the collective mind. However, everyone draws their thoughts from the same one source. Freedom of the mind is what is called for here in order to move around. You know your personal thoughts and beliefs, but you are free to explore others as well.

Continuing up through the chakras leads to the Sixth Chakra and imagination. Again, since it is an upper chakra, it deals with the collective image bank from which everyone draws images. To gain freedom here actually requires some discipline. Without discipline, the imagination appears free, but it is most often led by compulsions and habits with periodic glimpses of creativity and inspiration. With discipline, one can learn to discriminate between healthy and unhealthy expressions, learn to disengage from unhealthy wanderings, and direct the imagination toward creative and inspirational images.

We finally arrive at the Crown, or Seventh, Chakra. This is where the connection to the sense of oneness can be experienced. The spirit of humanity. The spirit that animates all of life. The great oneness that has been known by many names, but in truth, can't be named. A name would limit it, and it encompasses all limitations. Freedom here requires you to move beyond the personal experience and surrender to the transcendent life force of Divine Will. If you personalize the experience, you may think you are God, or you may think you are insane. Both are excessive attachments to the experience. To be free of these requires one to "let go and let God." This freedom is based on faith—faith that the life force which pulses beyond the self is benevolent, and you will be safe by surrendering into it.

Remember, knowing about the chakras is not the same as experiencing the chakras. To directly experience the chakras, meditation is required. There can be spontaneous experiences of each of the chakras that happen outside of meditation, but to ground yourself with each of them, meditation is the preferred route.

Vows and the Chakras

IT IS INTERESTING to consider the traditional vows of the spiritual path in regard to the chakras. Traditionally, when one enters a commitment to a spiritual path, there are vows to take. No matter what the tradition, the vows are most often "poverty," "chastity," and "obedience." It would be interesting to see which chakra each of the vows relate to. Poverty would have to be associated with the First Chakra and its focus on survival. Chastity is obviously a renouncing of the Second Chakra of sexual pleasure. Obedience could go nowhere other than a renunciation of the Third Chakra of power.

It can be seen that the vows of poverty, chastity and obedience are a renunciation of the first three chakras. In our current work of trying to activate and align all of the chakras, renunciation would not be considered an ideal. When you renounce or repress part of your natural character, it doesn't go away, it just resurfaces in another way. In all fairness to traditional spiritual paths, I'm sure the intent is honorable: Shift one's attention away from the physical and toward the spiritual.

In theory this sounds great, but in practice, it leaves much to be desired. To begin with, there is the judgment that the upper chakras are good and the lower ones are bad. This lack of acceptance of the Divine nature of all parts of our being throws us into the world of duality. Good/bad: this part of me is good, this part of me is bad. Ultimately, this leads to shame, guilt, denial, projection, and a host of other troubles for the human soul.

One beautiful aspect of our current spiritual revolution is the attempt to move beyond duality and judgment by accepting all aspects of our being as our Divine birthright. Instead of renouncing the lower chakras, it is encouraged to honor them; to engage them as part of the total blessing of life, but not to get stuck in them. We saw in our exploration of the chakras that the lower ones are insatiable when focused on exclusively. This is why the traditions renounce them as they do. They do not want their followers to get stuck there. To engage the lower chakras, while simultaneously staying aware of the upper chakras, is the dance that allows movement throughout the system.

As above, so below. This is one of the most common axioms of the consciousness path. The microcosm reflects the macrocosm. When we consider conditions in the macrocosm, specifically how humanity treats Earth, it is easy to see how the philosophy of renouncing the physical body ultimately leads to a lack of respect for the physical body of the planet. If we teach that the physical is irrelevant and should be ignored in favor of the spiritual, is it any wonder that a spin-off of this is the wanton disregard for our physical environment? Our Western culture is not particularly spiritual, it is more mental, but it certainly demonstrates this same disregard for the physical as witnessed by our deteriorating environment.

For so long our spiritual traditions have taught that being in a body on earth is evidence of the fall from Divine

Vows and the Chakras

grace. If you were really good, you wouldn't be here. Christians teach the afterlife; if you are really good, you will get to heaven. Buddhists teach nirvana; if you are really good, you will reach nirvana. Hindus teach that if you are really good, you will get off the wheel of death and rebirth and not have to come back here. In all of these traditions, what is the not-so-subtle implication of life here on earth?

Perhaps we have been too arrogant and have not been able to see that life on earth is a gift. Many people have told me, quite reverently, that this is their last life on earth. I always wonder, where do they think they are going? To me, the cosmic joke is: "What if planet earth is the jewel in the entire universe?" What if our life here is a blessing and not something to be overcome? If we believed this, we would likely see all of life as sacred.

What if planet earth is the only planet with trees, birds, kisses, warm breezes and chocolate? What if my friends who are wishing themselves away from this planet end up on some sulfur-ridden planet in a future life with faint memories of flowers, friends, bodies and affection? How do we know *this* isn't the gift? Isn't it rather arrogant to look upon this planet and to assume we could do a better job of creation?

It is easy to point at the problems, the pollution, the suffering, and to say things here are certainly bad. But perhaps we should take a look at our religions and philosophies that judge the physical as bad and start making the connection to how these beliefs affect our collective actions.

It might seem like a big leap to connect ecological issues to a study of the chakras, but we want to remember the premise of the metaphysical path: Everything is interrelated. Does then the teaching that we have been kicked out of the garden of Eden have something to do with the way we relate to our planet? You bet it does! Does the renunciation of the physical chakras have something to do with our neglect of the planet? You bet it does. Choose to enter the garden. Refuse to be kicked out of Eden.

"Let there be peace on earth and let it begin with me," one of our spiritual sayings goes. It is as good a starting point as any. As we bring our physical bodies into alignment with our spiritual consciousness; as we learn to integrate mind, body, spirit and soul; as we learn to honor our physical bodies by allowing them to celebrate with prosperity, sexuality and power; as we allow our soul to have an abundance of heartfelt love; as we allow our upper chakras to help us to awaken to creativity, intuition and spirituality; as this dance of ego, soul and spirit becomes a celebration within our being; as we see ourselves connected to the entire biosphere, which is Gaia—then we will likely see a shift in policies that honor our planet rather than desecrate it.

Transmuting Energy

ENERGY IS ENERGY. It cannot be repressed, nor neutralized, but it can be transmuted from one polarity to another. We are all familiar with negative energy such as anger, frustration and irritation. J. Krishnamurti, in his book *Think on These Things,* has a chapter called "Creative Frustration." In this chapter, he discusses the concept that frustration is energy and can be worked with for our benefit. As energy, in and of itself, it is not necessarily bad. It is when it is locked into a negative reaction that the problems tend to erupt.

He writes the first and foremost necessary step in transmuting energy is letting go of the label of its source. Instead of being mad because of what he said or she said, or they did, let go of the label and simply be mad. Essentially, we give away our power when we *identify the source as external to us.* If I am mad because of what he said, etc., I have given the power to the label. I have defined to my subconscious that I am powerless in this situation. The source of power is outside of me. What he said is the all powerful source that caused my anger. With this labeling, I have no power—I have given it away to what he said. With this labeling, there is nothing I can do with the energy, because I have defined myself as powerless in the situation. By renouncing the label and claiming the source of the experience *within myself*, I have regained a position of power with the energy. It is my anger, not because of anything. It simply *is*. Without attachment to the label, the anger is now in a usable form. It can now be transmuted.

I like to add visualization and chakra work to help transmute the energy. Here is the exercise. First, just as Krishnamurti suggests, it is necessary to let go of the label, or the reason why I think I am experiencing anger, frustration, irritation, etc. The ego will still attempt to come up with a label, as its job is to rationalize and develop a reason for the experience at hand. I remind myself that if it wasn't the current issue, it would be a hundred other reasons. So first I simply own the energy by saying "I am mad" . . . or angry, upset, irritated, or whatever.

Then I visualize this energy as a dark ball of negative energy low in my chakras, in the base of my spine. Next I let go of this image and move into my Heart Chakra where I visualize a ball of fiery energy. I engage a few deep breaths to pump up the energy and see the fire of my Heart Chakra burning brightly.

Next I return to the image of the dark ball of energy at the base of my spine. Then I breathe into this negative energy and, on the in-breath, I picture pulling this dark ball of energy up my spine. As it becomes engulfed in the fiery ball of energy, I see all the darkness of this energy burned away by the fire in my heart.

It has now become clear radiant energy, unattached to anything. Now I have the same amount of energy, but it is liberated from the reactionary state, and I can express it as I

Transmuting Energy

choose. I can work in my garden, write a book, get involved in a workout, or anything else I choose. The energy has been transmuted from its negative reaction to positive creative energy which can be directed at will.

Adversary vs. Visionary Views

AN ADVERSARIAL VIEW of life motivates most people. This is looking at life as if it were a constant test. Problems are seen that must be overcome. Challenges are encountered, and one must find a solution. Life is tough, and only those able to overcome the trials and tribulations are able to survive. There is energy in this view of life. Believing life is out to get you is definitely motivational. The problem with this view of life is that it is exhausting. It eventually wears you down to be constantly on guard against the next adversary. Consciousness that is centered in the first three chakras will look at life in this competitive manner.

A visionary view looks at life from a different perspective. Instead of "have to," it is "get to." When you raise your consciousness to a visionary level, you draw on inspiration as the primary motivating force instead of drawing on the energy from facing challenges. It is a complete paradigm shift. You then look at life as opportunities instead of challenges to be overcome. To get to the visionary level of life, you must rise above the reactionary tendencies of the lower chakras, and center your attention in the upper chakras.

This shift from an adversary to a visionary view of life does take some effort. Without effort, you would operate from a reactionary view of a survivalist, which our culture seems to promote. You cannot defeat the adversarial view and ultimately win, as this prospect, in and of itself, is an adversarial view! Instead of finally winning the game of survival, you simply learn to direct your attention to the upper chakras. By attending to the upper levels of consciousness, inspiration comes. It is not quite like thinking about visionary issues, it is more like residing in the upper chakras, then visionary inspiration simply comes to you.

It is entering the void and then discovering that it is not a void at all. Like the explorers of the fifteenth and sixteenth centuries, who had to have faith to go beyond the mapped world and trust they would not fall off, explorers in consciousness must have faith to go beyond their known world, believing other levels of life will be there waiting for them. The unknown world is far more vast than the known world, and to become a visionary in consciousness you must be willing to enter into the vast unknown.

Try living it. You have to learn to thrive in a non-adversarial view of life. How long can you live without anger and frustration? It is harder than it sounds because there is not built-in energy as there is with reactions to problems. How long can you live without frustration, anger and irritation? How long can you stay in a place of peace in yourself? How long can you wake up in the morning with creative ideas animating your energy rather than enemies or problems to overcome? It is harder than it sounds because there are always plenty of justifiable reasons to stay in the reactionary lower three chakras.

It is said that it is easy to stay centered on a mountain top, but very difficult to maintain this centered consciousness in

Adversary vs. Visionary Views

the world. Does this mean the ideal is to become totally passive in all life? Certainly not. Each of us will be confronted with many issues in life that call for a passionate, intense response. We are not talking about disengaging from the lower three chakras, simply not being *dominated* by them. There are times when we do need to make a stand about what we believe in. Our values and honor code will get tested—that seems to be part of life, but you can make a stand for what you believe in a non-adversarial way.

Problems do arise—relationships, work, life, all of these interactions are certain to lead to occasional conflicts. The visionary person works through these troubled times smoother, easier, and quicker than the adversarial person. You can listen to the whispers, or listen to the shouts. As you shift toward the visionary life, you perceive the subtle whisper of problems as they begin to arise. Subtle adjustments work for subtle problems. Wait until the problem announces itself as a shout, and the trauma/drama lifestyle is sure to follow.

Playing the Synthesizer of Your Being

THE CHAKRA SYSTEM is like a musical synthesizer. Each of the separate chakras is like a distinct note. Although separate, they can also be played in various combinations. Of course, it would be grand to be fully activated in all the chakras, but we do not live on mountain tops, we live in the valleys of reality. Each situation we engage in life provides a unique opportunity for blending and synthesizing various chakras.

A common example of synthesizing chakras is the pre-performance visualization so often promoted in sports these days. It has been verified that if a person can visualize the perfect shot ahead of time, it helps to promote that actuality. It is not 100 percent, of course, but it does obviously help. To use this principle, a person about to serve a tennis shot would first visualize the experience and enter into the feeling of a successful serve. This greatly improves the likelihood of actually hitting one. Compare this to the person who fears making a bad shot and clearly visualizes this eventuality. This obviously increases the likelihood of the bad shot.

I have spent a great deal of time coaching little league baseball. In teaching young players how to hit a baseball, I had the opportunity to see this principle in action. For the kids who had a difficult time hitting the ball, I could see their fear as they stepped up to the plate. Their biggest concern was to not strike out. They would be consumed by the fear of this and would approach hitting with the hope of not missing the ball.

The problem was clear. Their minds were focused on the fear of missing the ball, and this would increase its likelihood. I would encourage them not to focus on this fear, but instead go up to the plate with the hope of hitting the ball. I encouraged them to see the players on the field and to picture in their minds where they would want to hit the ball. Instead of their focus being on not striking out, they changed the picture in their minds to intending to hit the ball and, of course, this increased their success.

This same technique has just as positive results in other activities as well, for if it can work in sports, the principle works and can be applied in other areas just as successfully. How many situations, on a regular basis, do we find ourselves in where the outcome can be influenced by whether we react with fear or faith? This goes beyond simply maintaining a positive attitude.

The positive mental attitude approach to life is still just an approach. The type of visualization I am encouraging goes beyond approach, because it is an actual feeling, in the present moment, of the positive outcome of the event. You visualize the desired outcome and enter into the feeling of the success in present time. You are not just hoping things will turn out, you are experiencing the emotion *as if they already have manifested*. I call this "entering into the feelings of the eventual success."

Watch the principle work in its negative manifestation when you go into an experience with trepidation or fear. Here is the actual laboratory. Can you use your spiritual

Playing the Synthesizer of Your Being

will to pull your attention away from the fear and toward faith? Can you go one step further and imagine the experience in front of you coming to successful completion? Can you go one step further and feel in your body the experience of having successfully completed the experience before you? Can you go one step further and experience the felt sense of the success of your experience in the present time and hold onto that vision? These are the steps to take in actualizing this into daily life.

When I was in graduate school, I applied this technique in my test-taking strategies. Like everyone else, I would study and cram the night before a test or important paper that was due the next day. However, while the other students would continue cramming right up to the moment of the test, I would spend the half hour before the test meditating. I would first center myself with breath and focus on the chakras. Then I would visualize taking the test, turning it in to the professor, see him grade it and hand it back to me with a high score and a congratulations on a job well done. I would imagine what this success would feel like, then I would enter into that emotional feeling and feel it in present time. I would feel the satisfaction of a job well done in present time and hold onto that vision as I took the test. It helped considerably and consistently lead to a successful outcome.

Stages of Prayer

WE OFTEN PRAY for others, as well we should. Family members that are sick or troubled can benefit from our prayers. We often pray for the well-being of those suffering on the planet. Again, it's good to send a blessing for those who are less fortunate than us. To make prayers more effective, it is advisable to first bring the Divine Presence into our own life. We cannot give to others what we do not have ourselves.

To send effective prayers to others, first take responsibility for aligning with spirit in such a way that you can feel the Divine Presence in your being. Visualize the Divine Emanations coming down through the Crown Chakra and all the way down into your personal chakras, the first three. After you have felt this Divine Presence in your being, then you can effectively send this Divine energy to those you love.

When sending a prayer to a specific person, picture the energy emanating from your Heart Chakra to facilitate this process. Then you can continue up the chakras to the upper, collective chakras to send your prayers out into the collective. When sending prayers to humanity, see this emanating from your Crown Chakra.

If you wanted to be a philanthropist and give money to worthy causes, yet you were broke, your altruism would only be a good idea at best. In order to be effective, you would first have to acquire resources in order to have something to give. It is the same with prayer. When you pray for others without first inviting the Divine into your own life, it is only a good idea. You cannot do harm, but you cannot do what you are intending until you first fill yourself with spirit and then give from this wellspring.

Worry as Energy

IT IS APPROPRIATE to discuss worry at this time in relation to the power of prayer. Prayer works because the principle works. When we send our energy to others, it has an impact in proportion to the quality of energy we are sending.

Recently, one of my friends was deathly sick. It looked like death was certain, so much so the doctors had called in his family to say goodbye to him. This was a much loved man who had quite a positive impact in the lives of many people. The word of his impending death spread through the entire community, which responded by forming prayer circles. These were totally cross-cultural: Catholics, Buddhists, Protestants, New Age groups and members of the business community who were not religious, all got together and prayed for our friend's well-being. A miracle happened—he lived. The doctors couldn't believe this because they had never seen anybody come back from as far into death as he was. The power of prayer clearly worked.

What is worry in relation to this principle? It is negative prayer. It is literally sending negative energy and wrapping others in our fears. An illustration might be helpful. What is the color of worry? Black? Grayish green? Mucky brown?

What is the tone, the sound of worry? A heavy minor tone? Imagine getting a canvas out ready to paint on. Now imagine playing the sounds of worry in the background to set the mood while getting the colors out that you associate with worry.

Imagine yourself painting a picture with these colors that captures the feelings of your worry. Imagine getting the picture framed and then wrapping the painting up as a gift. Imagine sending the painting to someone that you worry about with a note that says "This is my gift to you. Hang this painting somewhere where you can see it often, and when you look at it and capture the feeling of the painting, realize this is how I am holding you in my thoughts." What kind of gift is that? Would the person for whom you are worrying appreciate it as a gift?

The illustration is a wake-up call for those of you who were raised to believe that it is good to worry for those you love. Consider the quality of the energy that you are sending to your loved ones. Isn't this just like negative prayer? Instead of sending love, light and Divine Energy, you are sending dark, fear-based energy to the ones you love. Remember, if the power of prayer works, the power of worry works in a negative way. If the principle works, it works in both its positive and negative polarities. Take responsibility for the quality of energy you send to others.

Some worry is going to happen, particularly if you have children. Of course you will worry some—the point isn't to feel guilty; no, the point is to realize that this activity is not helping anyone. Try to minimize your time with worry; when it arises, note it for what it is and choose not to dwell on it. Move your images to what you want to see and away from what you don't want to see manifest.

Worry as Energy

I've heard of an American Indian tradition called the "Worry Basket." In this tradition, if you were going to visit others in their lodge, you would pick up a few sticks along the way representing your worries. There would be a worry basket at the door of the lodge and you would put your sticks into the basket before entering. You wouldn't bring your worries in with you. When you left, you would reclaim your issues by taking your worry sticks with you.

I like this image—it provides a method for dealing with the worries that do arise. Let's expand on this image from not just the lodges of others, but where you visit them within yourself as well. When you think about someone, first place your worries in a basket in your mind. It's not that you don't have worries, you know you do. But you make these your issue and don't project them onto others.

Honoring Your Energy

YOU HAVE TO start from where you are; that is obvious enough. To honor your energy is to start with where you are now and all that got you this far. Honor your current energy patterns, including your addictions, habits, negative traits, petty issues, and everything else about the current truth of who you are. Start from here. We all are human, and we all have human frailties—our behavior patterns that we are not particularly proud of. This is part of our humanity.

To honor your energy as is, start by not judging your humanity. If you hold the belief that you'll know when you are making progress on your path by seeing your negative traits and neurotic tendencies disappear, you will never make progress! We'll always have our current stuff to work on. As we awaken to our higher selves, the issues become more subtle, but they still come.

One of my favorite sayings, if you'll forgive my crudeness, is: "enlightened today, asshole tomorrow!" We never escape our humanity, and when it arises, try to be as compassionate with yourself as you would be with others dealing with their human issues.

This disempowers your issues. When you hold their absence as the all-powerful clue of your progress, you have given them way too much power. Take your judgments about yourself off the pedestal and bring them down to a human level. It's just your stuff, like everybody else has their stuff, this is part of your agenda. It's not off your path to be working with your petty issues; it's simply part of it.

When jealousy, envy, petty anger, judgments, etc., arise, see them as the current field of consciousness that your soul needs to work with at this time. Instead of being distraught for having the petty issues in the first place, you see them as the current issues your soul needs you to work on for your growth. By accepting your issues, they are easier to tame and will continue to become increasingly more subtle.

Kundalini

KUNDALINI IS A principle from Hindu philosophy that is helpful for understanding this process of moving the energy up through the chakras. Basically, Kundalini means "serpent power." Kundalini energy is coiled at the base of the spine. Through different situations, exercises and meditations the kundalini uncoils and moves up the series of chakras, releasing the energy stored in each chakra it contacts. This method of visualization offers us an image of understanding the process of awakening to the surge of energy released in the upper chakras.

Kundalini experiences can happen spontaneously, where you simply seem to fall into the release of this incredible energy—quite by chance. To experience the surges of energy of the upper chakras is one thing when that is what you are trying to do, but it is quite another thing when a person has no preparation or training for handling the awakened energy. Most often, when people are talking about Kundalini energy, it is problematic. Crazy energy: rushes, twitches, heat, anxiety attacks, too much energy. These are all clues the energy isn't being balanced.

The Kundalini has risen beyond the ability to handle the energy and the crazy energy is essentially a "shooting out" of uncontrolled energy. When it is balanced, it is integrated and decidedly not phenomenological. There is not an outer display because the energy isn't being thrown off, it's becoming integrated.

To raise the Kundalini to its highest potential it is necessary to balance the expression of it at each successive chakra, starting at the Root Chakra. You can open up to a higher chakra experience, even if you are unbalanced in a lower one, but you cannot sustain the higher level—the needs of the unbalanced chakra will pull your attention down to experiences connected to the needs of the unbalanced chakra. When the needs of a chakra become balanced, the Kundalini energy naturally and spontaneously rises to the next-higher energy center.

A Myth

WE ARE THE Counsel of Seven and you will be hearing more from us as more of you awaken to full consciousness. We are nothing more than the collective wisdom of humanity. As each of you awaken to full consciousness, and your role within humanity, our voice gets stronger. To listen to our guidance the rules are simple—that which unites will lead you to us and that which separates will lead you astray. To listen to the universal mind, adopt a universal philosophy. We would like to tell you a story.

A long, long time ago, when we were all still light beings existing in spirit but not in form, our tribe of angels was exploring the universe for opportunities to serve. We were on a fly-by of planet earth and noticed all the suffering occurring there. Here was a planet of tremendous beauty beyond compare in all of the universe, yet it was encased in a shroud of fear that limited the inhabitants in their ability to realize what a gift their lovely planet was.

Our leaders looked down upon the situation and, with compassion, thought this was a planet that certainly needed cosmic assistance to bring it into the love vibration. It was suggested that perhaps we would like to go down to earth and dwell within the life forms that were already existing there and see if we could assist the evolution of the planet toward love. Volunteers were asked for, and we naively accepted the assignment, believing that it would not be difficult to bring awareness to the tremendous beauty that was all around.

Preparations were made by our leaders to influence the genetic make-up of the most likely species, humans. This took thousands of years, which in earth time seemed painfully slow, yet in cosmic time, was a blink of an eye. The brain and consciousness of the human species had to be retooled through DNA encoding to become suitable hosts for the incoming spirits. When the consciousness was sufficiently evolved, the first emissaries were sent to begin the process of leading the planet out of fear. Our leaders planned for this well and even left maps of how to return to our celestial origins. The intent was to bring each body together with a guardian angel that would lead to a marriage of heaven on earth. The beginning stages of the experiment went marvelously well. The bodies received the spirit and, just as predicted, the veil of forgetfulness dropped over the spirit as it became enmeshed in the fascinating world of the senses.

The plan was that spirit dwelling within the people would become hungry to reunite with its celestial identity and the remembering of its purpose would begin. What wasn't planned for was when spirit entered into the body, fertilization occurred, and the soul was born from this union. The soul was not just allegiant to spirit, it was equally attached to the human form and the delightful world of the senses. Relationships, love, intimacy, and the agonies along the way nurtured the soul. Spirit was trying to break free of the human condition, but soul was very much aligned with the lessons of being human.

Many maps of the journey back home were provided: religions of every sort and kind, something for every attitude and cultural heritage. The wisdom teachings were spread through all of the cultures so that everyone would be able to find a path. All of the paths, if followed with the highest intent, would lead spirit back home to the source—oneness. However, these maps became perverted by the fear-encased mentality of the planet, so the first uses of these various religions and paths held people in their fears instead of liberating them. All that unites furthers, all that separates hinders. The religions drifted toward separatist ways, each disbelieving in the validity of other paths. The very tools which were meant to liberate people, instead further tied them to separatist ways.

Our leaders had all the time in the universe and continued to work toward influencing the consciousness of the planet to pull attention to the celestial levels. This was done by quickening the electromagnetic energy field. They seeded the ideas that would lead to the invention of materials that would break down the ozone layer, allowing higher frequency vibrations into the atmosphere, shifting the electromagnetic energy field toward a higher vibration. The scientists still trapped in a fear-based mentality saw the breakdown of the ozone layer as further evidence to fear nature. However, more and more individuals started awakening to the higher levels of consciousness available in the higher frequency energy fields.

These individuals became the visionaries. They saw the spiritual intention behind each of the maps, paths and religions is to liberate individuals from a fear-based reality. By inviting their higher selves and guardian angels into their lives, they were able to liberate themselves from the ego-encapsulated view of life. They found the way to use the paths to identify specific karmic indicators that the soul needed to deal with, heal and integrate, and this healing was not difficult with the assistance of spirit.

At first, these visionaries were accused of being "airy-fairy," ungrounded in reality, space cadets, until they were able to demonstrate their truth. As more and more individuals successfully used the maps to heal old wounds and move into cooperation with spirit, the example of their lives became a model of what was possible. The demonstration of a life guided by spirit and nurtured by soul grew, and these visionaries became living examples that others could follow. Their love was so much stronger than fear, that once these individuals woke up to the full remembrance of their purpose, they became as a light in the darkness that could help others to see.

This story need not be a fairy tale. We do tremendous service by advising others of their possibilities, but the greatest legacy that we will leave behind is the life we live ourselves. Physician, heal thyself. Live your truth. If we are to be a powerful influence in healing this planet, then it is we ourselves that must demonstrate this in how we live our lives. We have the maps for integration. We can live a life of health in body, mind, spirit and soul. By doing so, we are grounding the vision of our spiritual leaders and creating a light for others to follow.

Section IV
Exercises and Meditations

Visualization Exercise

MOST OFTEN I prefer to use meditation and visualizations for aligning with the energy I want to experience. There are, however, methods for using visualization to remove unwanted energies. The following is a good example for doing just that.

Exercise 11

For Filtering Out Unwanted Energies: First get in a meditative state and activate each of the chakras through one of the chakra meditations. Next, visualize a screen in front of you, like a large screen door. Then, imagine yourself moving through that screen and imagine that all unwanted energies attached to you—worries, fears, expectations from others, etc., are filtered out as you move through the screen.

As you picture yourself on the other side of the screen, feel what it is like to be your most genuine self without any unnatural energies attached to you. Walk through another screen in your mind's eye with even a finer mesh and see yourself purified of all that is not your true essence. Walk through as many screens as it takes until you see the colors of your aura as pure, and radiating a brilliant light.

Chakra Meditation

THIS MEDITATION IS designed to focus your awareness upon each of the chakra centers. The intent is to feel the energy associated with each of the chakras and to cleanse the passageways connecting each center.

To begin, find a quiet spot in which to sit. Make certain that your spine is straight, and you are comfortable enough to maintain the same position for fifteen to twenty minutes. When you feel calm, with each in-breath, visualize a beam of white light entering your body through the top of your head. Follow this light as it travels down your spine. Feel its energy collect at the base of the spine as you hold your breath. With each out-breath, visualize the energy traveling back up your spine. As it passes through each chakra, visualize the energy getting darker as it cleanses away the impurities. When it finally leaves through the crown of the head, picture it having a dark, muddy color. Complete this process several times and with each successive attempt, see your energy becoming a clearer and cleaner emanation from the Crown Chakra.

Now you are ready to start focusing on the revitalization of each of the separate chakras. (Your eyes should remain closed throughout the entire meditation.) Breath is the key. Mystics know that you can breathe anything into your being: Love, clarity, wisdom, courage. You focus on the issue and, on the in-breath, you imagine breathing that energy into your being. Hold your breath for a slow count of four and feel the energy fill your being. Breathe it in, hold it and let it fill your being, then emanate it outward with the out-breath. In this meditation we will be using colors, so breathe the color in, hold it and let it fill your being and then breathe it out and feel that color emanating from your being.

First Chakra

Draw the beam of white light down to the base of the spine. Hold this light in your First Chakra and visualize it turning a deep red. Hold your breath and focus on the physical nature of your senses. Feel yourself become passionate, strong, physical, and filled with courageous energy. As you breathe out, emanate the color red and feel its strength. Do this a few cycles until you enter into the feeling of the First Chakra.

Second Chakra

Again breathe the beam of white light to the base of your spine. Follow the energy up to the next chakra, located just above the pubic ridge. Visualize the energy becoming a deep orange color. While you bathe in this color, allow yourself to feel a sense of vitality and vigor. Recognize yourself as magnetic and know that you can attract to you all you need. Feel your sensuality awaken as your five senses come alive and, as you breathe out, send this magnetic, joyous energy out into the world.

Third Chakra

First, bring the beam of white light down to the base of your spine. Then, let it continue its upward journey to the area two-to-three inches above your navel, known as the solar plexus. Visualize the color changing to a brilliant yellow. Know yourself as a person endowed with independent choice in the expression of your will. Feel the clarity of your personal power, feel it firmly rooted in the values and convictions that you believe in. Feel yourself enter into a sense of total independence and breathe this clarity into the world.

Fourth Chakra

Bring the white light to the root chakra and let it move up to the area of the heart and visualize a rich forest-green color emanating from the heart. As you surround yourself with this refreshing ray, realize you are a totally loving, accepting person. Feel the abundance of life and know there is plenty of everything for everybody. Awaken to your generosity and share your heart with the world. Know that you can make decisions from your heart that will unite both your personal and spiritual needs.

Fifth Chakra

Bring the white ray to the base of your being and let it rise upward to your throat and immerse yourself in a sky-blue light. Let your thoughts be as boundless as the sky; allow your imagination to carry your vision to endless reaches of awareness. Awaken to your ability to view the world creatively and your capacity to express your true self. Awaken to your authentic self, liberated from cultural conditioning.

Sixth Chakra

Follow the white light into your First Chakra and then let it rise through each of the chakras up to your Third Eye at the brow. Let the beam of light transform to the color indigo blue as you focus upon the space between your eyes. Feel the wisdom of acceptance of life as it is. This leads to a sense of oneness with all life. From this perspective, you can see both your life from a worldly view and simultaneously see it from a larger, spiritual perspective. Judgments drop as you simply become a witness to your life. You are entering into your bliss as you feel aligned with a larger flow of life that is not of your making. Be aware of the penetrating insights that come from your intuition.

Seventh Chakra

One last time you trace the movement of the white light down through the chakras and, this time, let it rise to your Crown Chakra and out. Picture a violet glow surrounding you and, as you hold your breath, fill yourself with this light. Realize that you are no longer alone as a separate being; you are one with all. Feel the sense of spiritual protection as you align with the Divine. Breathe out and send the energy of your being to the Divine and the world around you.

With your eyes still closed, begin to sense that you are sitting in the room. Again become aware of surrounding noises and smells. Still keeping your breathing regular, open your eyes and notice the refreshing awareness of NOW.

Heaven and Earth Meditation

SIT IN A comfortable meditation posture. Any posture that the spine is straight: lotus posture, in a chair, against a wall, or even lying down. Center yourself by focusing on your breath. Notice the in-breath and the out-breath. Notice the subtle rising in your being on the in-breath. Notice the subtle falling in of your being on the out-breath. Notice the changing of the breaths. See if you can even become aware of the sound of the subtle click in-between breaths. Ah, *center*.

Now practice playing the scales of your chakra system by focusing on each one in turn. Start with the First Chakra. Feel it by drawing your attention to it and see the color red and feel the attributes connected to this center. Move up through each of the chakras in succession by focusing on the appropriate colors (red, orange, yellow, green, blue, indigo, violet) and attributes. Then move back down the chakras from the Crown to the Root Chakra. Do this a few times, like playing the scales on a piano.

Next, imagine your spine extending down through the floor and into the earth. See roots growing out of the base of this extended spine, deep into the earth. See these roots entangling with the roots of the great trees and draw this centered, grounded strength all the way up through the earth and into your heart. Feel this rooted, connected, secure feeling in your heart.

Next, imagine your spine extending up through the crown of your head, up through the ceiling and into the heavens. See your extended spine as a huge antenna branching out into the heavens. Feel this antenna capturing the spiritual energy flowing through the cosmos. Imagine yourself drawing this energy down from the heavens and into your heart. Feel this spiritual energy in your heart.

Now, visualize both simultaneously. Draw the energy up from the earth and down from the heavens simultaneously and feel them merge in your heart. On your in-breath, draw this energy from both heaven and earth. Hold your breath for a few seconds and feel this energy collecting and merging in your heart. This is the energy of heaven on earth. On your out-breath, see this energy radiating from your being out into the world. Breathe in, breathe out. Draw this energy to you and send it out into the world.

APPENDIX

Chakra Chart

Chakra	Drive	Core Issue	Perspective
1	*survival*	find place on earth	animal instinct; separate sense of self
2	*pleasure*	sensuality/sexuality	emotional self
3	*power*	will power; initiate activities and set boundaries	principles; what you stand for
4	*love*	open heart to all; non-competitive	cooperation
5	*creativity*	speak your truth	unique world-view beyond cultural conditioning
6	*transcendence*	be an inspiration to others	transcend polarities; insightful
7	*spirituality*	connecting with Divine intent	seeing through the eyes of the Divine

APPENDIX: Chakra Chart

Level of Consciousness	Unbalanced	Task
safety; connection to body and earth	insecurity	to be fully in the body
awareness of magnetic energy	hedonistic/indulgent	to enjoy life
looking for opportunities for assertion of will	power conflicts	learn to choose wisely
being at peace	bleeding heart	joy
detach and observe without bias, then synthesize varying views	inadequacy or insensitivity	to be authentic
intuitive inner guidance from aligning with larger reality	spacing out; illusions	to be able to direct imagination
experiencing all of life as spiritual	"shopping list" mentality	surrender

REFERENCES AND SUGGESTED READING

Bach, Richard. *Illusions.* New York, NY: Dell, 1977.

Barks, Coleman. *The Essential Rumi.* San Francisco, CA: Harper, 1995.

Blum, Ralph. *The Book of Runes.* New York, NY: St. Martins Press, 1982.

Brennan, Barbara. *Hands of Light.* New York, NY: Bantam Books, 1988.

Bridges, Carol. *The Medicine Woman Inner Guidebook.* Nashville, IN: Earth Nation Publishing, 1987.

Carey, Ken. *Return of the Bird Tribes.* San Francisco, CA: HarperCollins, 1988.

Chödrön, Pema. *When Things Fall Apart.* Boston, MA: Shambhala Publications, 1997.

———. *Start Where You Are.* Boston, MA: Shambhala Publications, 1994.

Coelho, Paulo. *The Alchemist.* San Francisco, CA: Harper, 1993.

Goldstein & Kornfield. *Seeking the Heart of Wisdom.* Boston & London: Shambhala, 1987.

Grof, Stanislav & Christina. *Spiritual Emergency.* Los Angeles, CA: Jeremy P. Tarcher, 1989.

Judith, Anodea. *Wheels of Life.* St. Paul, MN: Llewellyn, 1997. Revised edition, 1999.

Jung, C.G. *Memories, Dreams, Reflections.* New York, NY: Vintage Books, 1961.

———. *Modern Man in Search of a Soul.* New York, NY: Harcourt, Brace & World, 1933.

Krishnamurti, J. *Think on these Things.* New York, NY: HarperCollins, 1989.

Long, Max Freedom. *The Secret Science at Work.* Marina del Rey, CA: DeVorss & Co, 1953.

Marciniak, Barbara, *Bringers of the Dawn.* Santa Fe: Bear & Co. Inc., 1992.

Mitchell, Stephen. *Tao Te Ching.* New York, NY: Harper Perennial, 1991.

Moore, Thomas. *Care of the Soul.* New York, NY: HarperCollins, 1992.

Myss, Caroline, M. *Anatomy of Spirit.* New York: Harmony Books, 1996.

Pond, David & Lucy. *The Metaphysical Handbook.* Pt. Ludlow, WA: Reflecting Pond Publications, 1984.

Rajneesh, Bhagwan Shree. *The Book of Secrets.* New York, NY: Harper & Row, 1977.

Richardson/Huett. *Spiritual Value of Gem Stones.* Marina del Rey, CA: DeVorss & Co, 1980.

Rinpoche, Sogyal. *The Tibetan Book of Living and Dying.* San Francisco, CA: Harper, 1992.

Rodegast/Stanton. *Emmanuel's Book.* New York, NY: Bantam Books, 1989.

Sams & Carson. *Medicine Cards.* Santa Fe, NM: Bear & Company, 1988.

The Dali Lama. *The Power of Compassion.* London & San Francisco: Thorsons, 1995.

Villoldo, Alberto and Jendresen, Erik. *The Four Winds.* New York, NY: Harper and Row, 1990.

Walsch, Neale Donald. *Conversations with God.* New York, NY: G.P. Putman's Sons, 1996.

Wilhem, Richard. Translation by Cary Baynes. *The I Ching.* Princeton, NJ: Princeton University Press, 1950.

Yogananda, Paramahansa. *Autobiography of a Yogi.* Los Angeles, Self Realization Fellowship.

INDEX

abundance, 26–27, 30, 56, 58, 68, 122, 155
acceptance, 58, 117, 120, 156
adrenaline, 47
adversary, 127–129
alcohol, 35, 37, 84, 92
Alpert, Richard (see *Ram Dass*)
anger, 47–48, 70, 123–124, 128, 142
animal nature, 23, 30–31, 63
anxiety, 38, 72, 79, 143
appreciation, 34, 39–41
ashram, 84, 96
astral plane, 89–90
astrology, 110–111
attachment, 63, 65, 82, 92, 124
attention, 7, 12, 22–23, 27, 42, 53, 64, 68–69, 79, 85–86, 91, 93, 95, 99, 106, 119, 127–128, 133, 144, 147, 157
attractiveness, 38–39
authentic self, 71, 80, 105, 155

balance, 9–13, 15, 17, 25–26, 30–31, 34, 36–41, 48–50, 52–53, 57–58, 61–62, 78–79, 91, 96, 104, 108, 144
Beatles, the, 60
beauty, 3, 5, 38–39, 43, 59, 66, 69, 75, 145–146
Bhagavad Gita, 104
Bible, the, 104
bleeding heart, 61, 161
bliss, 57, 83, 88, 94, 105, 156
bodhisattva, 105
body, 4, 7, 11, 23–24, 28, 36, 39–41, 56, 84–85, 108,

120, 122, 133, 146, 148, 153, 161
boundaries, 45–46, 48, 160
breath, 79, 99, 133, 153–154, 156–158
Buddha, 108
Buddhists, 89, 105, 121
chakras,
   First (Root), 7, 15, 18, 23–31, 33, 41, 46, 52, 61, 64, 119, 144, 154–157
   Second (Sacral), 15, 19, 30–31, 33–43, 46, 52, 64, 93, 119, 154
   Third (Solar Plexus), 4, 18, 45–54, 58, 64–65, 74, 84, 119, 155
   Fourth (Heart), 15, 55–70, 115–116, 124, 135, 155
   Fifth (Throat), 71–83, 92, 117, 155
   Sixth (Third Eye), 83–99, 156
   Seventh (Crown), 7, 101–112, 118, 135, 153, 156
chastity, 119
chi (Qi), xii
Chocolate Cake Diet, the, 36
codependency, 61
collective consciousness, 82, 87, 89, 117
collective mind, 72–73, 77, 80, 86, 117
colors, 7, 22, 41, 151, 154, 157

compassion, 58, 63–64, 66, 69, 145
competition, 47, 50, 53, 57
conflict, 11–12, 47–48, 50–51, 53, 63, 69, 96, 98
convictions, 46, 155
cooperation, 50, 53, 58, 148, 160
creative blocks, 81
creative visualization (see *directed imagery*)
creativity, 15–16, 57, 71–73, 75–76, 79, 81–82, 86, 91, 96, 118, 122, 160
crystals, 22–23, 33, 45, 55, 71, 83, 101

deception, 76, 84
defenses, 26, 52, 56–57, 69, 116
desire, 33, 37, 39–40, 80, 83, 101
despair, 112
Dillon, Matt, 50
diplomacy, 53
directed imagery, 86
discernment, 45, 47, 51–52, 95
discovery, 74, 76
discrimination, 34, 46
divine discontent, 98–99
Divine, the, 24, 43, 60, 67, 83–84, 87–88, 92–94, 96–99, 101–109, 111–112, 118, 120–121, 135–136, 156, 160

INDEX

DNA, 146
drugs, 35, 37, 84, 92–93

earth, 3, 23–24, 28–29, 40, 67, 94, 117, 120–122, 145–146, 157–158, 160–161
effortless action, 12, 89
ego, 27, 51, 56, 75, 84, 104, 107, 109, 115–118, 122, 124
empathy, 63
environmental illness, 94
envy, 38, 41, 142
escapism, 83–84, 90–91
eternity, 105, 108
ethics, 45
exhaustion, 59, 67, 69

faith, 11, 16, 25, 29, 55–56, 68–69, 74, 84, 87–89, 91–92, 95, 98, 107–109, 111–112, 116, 118, 128, 132–133, 132–133
fantasy, 15, 84–85
fashion, 38
fear, 6, 25–26, 29–31, 37, 47, 55, 66, 68, 81, 84, 87–92, 95, 102, 104, 108, 132–133, 132–133, 145–148
forgiveness, 66
free will, 46
freedom, 5, 61, 76, 108, 117–118
frustration, 123–124, 128

Gaia, 117, 122
Gandhi, 108
generosity, 62, 155
God, 39, 98, 104, 106–107, 109, 118, 156, 160
Goddess, 104, 160
grace, 12, 57, 64, 67, 87, 102, 106, 121
grief, 63, 98
grounding, 28–29, 72, 104, 148
guilt, 42, 48, 63, 89, 92, 120
Gunsmoke (TV show), 50

habits, 63, 117, 141
Hanh, Thich, Nhat, 13, 108
harmony, 12, 15–19, 47, 50, 58, 60, 94
Harvard University, 82
heart, 4, 15, 27, 36, 43, 48, 55–70, 98, 115–116, 124, 135, 155, 158, 160–161
hedonism, 34
helplessness, 48
Hindu, 143
honor, 46, 51, 53, 81, 120, 122, 129, 141

I–Ching, 98
illusions, 84, 90, 161
images, 17, 43, 83, 85, 96, 117–118
imagination, 37, 83–87, 89–91, 93, 95, 117–118, 155, 161
inadequacy, 77, 161

indecision, 53
indulgence, 35–36
innovative thinking, 74
insecurity, 25–27, 41, 49, 161
insights, 72–75, 78, 80, 95, 156
inspiration, 59, 73, 83–84, 86, 90–92, 96–97, 107, 118, 127–128, 160
instincts, 12, 28–29, 31, 39, 91
integrity, 52
intellect, 45–46, 51
intentions, 52, 105
intuition, 15, 86, 95, 97, 122, 156

jealousy, 37, 41, 142
Jesus, 60, 108
joy, 55, 57–58, 62, 64–66, 116, 161
justifiable anger, 47–48

kindness, 64, 66
Koran, the, 104
Krishnamurti, 89, 123
kundalini, 143–144
Lao Tzu, 89, 108
Leary, Timothy, 82
Love, 15, 28, 34, 42–43, 55–57, 59–69, 93, 109, 122, 135, 145–146, 148, 154, 160
  Personal, 65–66
  Compassionate, 66–67
  Universal, 67–68

LSD, 82
lust, 28

magnetism, 33–34, 39–42, 52
manna, xi
martyr, 48
medicine cards, 98
meditation, 43, 81, 90, 99, 102, 118, 151, 153–158
mind, 11, 15, 29, 43, 47, 52, 54, 56, 72–80, 84–86, 89, 96, 117, 122, 145, 148, 151
mindfulness, 89
Mother Teresa, 108
Muktananda, 108

nature, 23–24, 27, 30–31, 38–39, 43, 53, 59, 61, 63, 69, 71, 78–80, 84, 87, 90, 96, 103, 120, 147, 154
need, 19, 25, 30, 33, 38–39, 47, 49–51, 53–54, 58–61, 71, 76, 97, 101, 103, 111–112, 116, 148, 154
nervousness, 72, 81

obedience, 119
obsessive, 40, 93
Olympic Peninsula, 111
Omega Institute, 82
options, 41, 80
oracles, 98
originality, 71
Osho, 58
overwhelmed, 54

passion, 30–31, 38, 110
patience, 108
peace, 13, 50, 57, 60, 69, 78, 96, 122, 128, 161
personal will, 74, 84, 89
personality, 56, 116
philosophy, 78, 120, 143, 145
pleasure, 15, 19, 33–36, 38–42, 46–47, 60, 119, 160
politics, 78
pornography, 40
poverty, 119
power, 15–16, 24, 31, 38, 45–47, 49–54, 60, 84, 105, 112, 119, 122–124, 142–143, 155, 160–161
power conflicts, 46–47, 49–50, 52, 161
pranna, xii
prayer, 11, 90, 102, 135–136
principles, 45–46, 52, 64, 160
problems, 61, 75–76, 116, 121, 123, 127–129
prophetic, 94
psychic, 94, 97
purpose, 22, 68–69, 80, 97–98, 103, 111, 146, 148

Ram Dass (Richard Alpert), 37, 70, 82
relationships, 41, 60, 86, 129, 146
renunciation, 34, 111, 119, 122
reverence, 102
romance, 42, 65

runes, 98

sacred, 98, 102, 104–105, 121
sacrifice, 56, 66, 84, 106–107
satisfaction, 13, 39, 41, 133
security, 15–16, 18, 25–28, 30, 41, 49, 51, 60–61, 110–111
self-confidence, 48
self-esteem, 48
self-knowledge, 74
sensitivity, 63, 93–94
sentimentality, 61
separateness, 25, 56, 65, 99
separation, 25, 30, 66, 92–93, 98
servant, 48
service, 48, 145, 148
sex, 23, 28, 35, 37, 60
shame, 48, 63, 89, 120
soul, 57, 66, 68–69, 80, 97, 103, 106–107, 111, 115–118, 120, 122, 142, 146, 148
spirit, 25, 30, 56, 67, 84–85, 88, 98, 107, 115–118, 122, 135–136, 145–148
spiritual, 6, 43, 55–56, 59, 61–62, 82–92, 95–99, 101–103, 105, 107–108, 110–111, 115, 119–120, 122, 133, 147–148, 155–156, 158, 161
spiritual practice, 95–96, 111
spiritual will, 84–87, 89–92, 95, 133

spirituality, 15, 101, 122, 160
sports, 29, 131–132, 131–132
stage fright, 77, 81
stress, 79
struggle, 53, 55, 64
suffering, 37, 63–64, 66–67,
    93–94, 98, 105, 107, 121,
    135, 145
surrender, 16, 42, 90,
    101–102, 104–106, 109,
    112, 118, 161
survival, 15, 17, 23–29, 34,
    46, 51, 57, 119, 128, 160

talking stick, 81
Tao, 88–89, 94, 104
Tao Te Ching, 89, 104
tape-loop thinking, 54
tarot cards, 98
television, 50, 84
third eye, 4, 94–96, 156
tranquillity, 15, 58
transcendence, 83–84, 90,
    160
transmuting energy, 123–125
truth, 46, 54, 71–73, 76–77,
    79, 81, 92, 108, 118, 141,
    148, 160

unconditional love, 60, 62, 67
universal energy, 3, 56, 59,
    67, 79
universal life force, 3, 5–6, 27,
    89, 95, 103
universal mind, 75, 145
Upanishads, the, 104

values, 27, 34, 36, 52,
    115–116, 129, 155
vision, 7, 62–63, 92, 96–98,
    133, 148, 155
visionary, 90, 96–97, 112,
    127–129
visualization, 28, 86, 124,
    131–132, 131–132, 143,
    151
voice, 71, 73–74, 86, 95–97,
    106, 110, 145
vows, 105, 119–122

will power, 160
wisdom, 34, 95, 97, 145, 147,
    154, 156
witness, 6–7, 18, 85, 89, 91,
    93–94, 156
Worry Basket, 139
worship, 90
writer's block, 81

yang energy, 67
yin energy, 67
yoga, 9, 12, 53, 81, 92, 96
Yogananda, 98, 108